THE UNITED STATES OF AMERICA, FREEDOM, LIBERTY, AND DEMOCRACY: A GUIDE TO UNDERSTANDING THE BATTLE BETWEEN LEFT AND RIGHT

Russell Hasan

CONTENTS

Title Page

Copyright

Preface

American History   1

Bunch of Crooks   8

The Right   16

The Left   22

Race and Gender   30

What is The Culture Wars?   37

Party Loyalty   40

The Libertarians and Objectivists   43

Is Libertarianism Left or Right?   52

Intro, Part II   56

The Left as Forced Feminization   58

The Right as Forced Masculinization   60

Libertarianism as Freedom   63

The Libertarian Hypothesis   66

Anti-Communism   70

Epilogue   81

PREFACE

This book is an explanation of The Culture Wars, which is the conflict between Left and Right, in the United States of America. What is at stake in this book is not merely abstract theory, but, perhaps, the potential to avoid a Second Civil War, or to avoid World War III. The book will argue that the Far Right and the Far Left are at war with each other, and, if either one were to defeat the other, each one intends to take power and achieve one-party rule. Only the patriotic love of freedom, and support for the United States Constitution, can save us from dictatorship, because it is the Constitution which would force the US government to put down an uprising by either the Far Left or the Far Right, thereby preserving our freedom.

That having been said, you should know, from page one, that this book is a work of scholarly abstract theory, in the domain of political science and philosophy. This is not a work of empirical research, nor is it a work of journalism. This book is not a manifesto, and does not support any particular party or politician.

Also, if you are not familiar with the author's other works, be made aware that he writes from a point of view situated within Libertarian politics and Objectivist philosophy. But he is known for a unique and original take on politics, which differs from what many other Libertarians and Objectivists believe.

The author is not a member of the political Right, and instead views himself as neither Left nor Right. Because of this, he is able to provide a neutral, unbiased, objective analysis of both Left and Right, being loyal to neither one.

Many people feel like it is too late for honesty, and feel that it has become impossible to understand the battle between Left and

Right, except by means of either a point of view that is biased in favor of the Left, or a point of view that is biased in favor of the Right. The objective truth, they think, has been destroyed. The central focus of this book is proving that mode of thinking wrong. It is not too late for honesty. It is not too late for the truth. This book tells the truth.

Portions of this book have previously appeared in other books by this author.

AMERICAN HISTORY

The foundational premise of the USA was that it would be a free democracy, whose central focus and guiding principle, as a society, was to be freedom. This was something that had not been tried since ancient Athens, and even the Greeks had not meant freedom in the full and total sense intended by the Americans.

The American vision of freedom was shaped by the ideas of the classical liberals, who had defined a liberal democracy as one in which there was liberty, in other words, freedom. By freedom, they meant that there would be no state religion, no state race, no state gender, and no state economy or state economics. No state religion meant that there would be no laws legislating morality. No state economics meant that there would be no laws legislating the economy. No state race or state gender meant that there would be no laws legislating race or gender.

There would be no state party, in other words, there would not be one political party favored by the state, in one-party rule. Instead, there would be freedom, so that things like religion, economics, and party, were chosen by the people, not imposed by force by the state.

The United States of America was never a perfect liberal democracy, from the start, and is not today. Slavery is one example of failure, although the Communist economics of FDR and JFK and LBJ are other examples. So there is no point in time at which this vision of liberal democracy was ever perfectly enacted. But liberal democracy is, and was, always the American ideal.

It was not a specifically or distinctly capitalist ideology, but there was a belief in rugged individualism, on the belief that the individual should be able to survive on their own, within the realm of economics and the physical world, but also within the realm of thought and ideas, by having a mind capable of making competent and intelligent independent judgments as an individual. They believed that the individual is competent to make choices, and, therefore, the individual should be free.

At the time, they called this a liberal democracy. The word liberal, used in this sense, meant of or related to liberty. Although most people today do not know this, the word liberal used to have a completely different meaning, in the 1700s and 1800s and early 1900s, so when I say liberal democracy, I mean classical liberal democracy. And, back then, when they spoke of liberal democracy, that was what they meant, too. A liberal democracy really meant a classical liberal democracy.

What the history teachers do not want you to know, and the reason why they changed the word liberal, is that classical liberalism used to be very popular in the Western world, in the USA and England and in many other places. Classical liberalism, in its ideas and ideals, is very close to modern libertarianism. So what the history teachers really do not want you to know, is that libertarianism is not really just a recent idea, and it has already played a huge role in American history and world history, and was responsible for some of humanity's greatest historical eras of peace, prosperity, and growth.

In order to maintain a liberal democracy, these people, the classical liberals, coined a new idea, the liberal arts education. The liberal arts education was intended to teach people the liberal arts, which means, those arts, skills, talents, and abilities, needed to live and thrive in a liberal democracy, which meant, in a democracy where the government was not going to take care of you and run your life for you, and where you would be on your own, and make your own decisions, and be responsible for yourself as a free and independent adult.

The liberal arts education included the ability to get a middle class job, with education in practical job skills and job training and career building. It was expected that each citizen would be able to get a middle class job, to have the money to take care of themselves without government help, so it was expected that a liberal arts education would teach the academic knowledge and career skills (and social skills) necessary to secure employment at a salary that could support a middle class life.

But it also included critical thinking skills, so that you could figure out which politicians you should vote for in a liberal democracy. The liberal arts education had to teach critical thinking skills so that you could tell which politicians were telling you the truth, and which were lying to you, so that you would know whom you should vote for, which it was expected would be necessary for liberal democracy to survive and flourish.

It was intended to be a well-rounded general education, so that you could contribute to civilization, as a well-educated member of society, in your liberal democracy.

Liberal democracy in the USA worked well, for about 200 years, in the 1800s and 1900s. It was an era of prosperity, growth, and freedom. The USA was neither a Christian state nor a Communist state. It was a liberal democracy.

Those on the Right who say that they want to return to the past, and resist or reverse change, by turning America into a Christian state, are factually and historically incorrect, because the USA never was a Christian state, at no point in time in American history. Ever since the Bill of Rights, there were clauses in the United States Constitution which explicitly forbade the creation of a Christian state, so America could never have been a Christian state, although there were politicians throughout history who tried to make it one, such as by making alcohol illegal through Prohibition.

Those on the Left, who say that America was always about equality and the fight against racism and slavery, and who cite this to say that a Communist state is American, are also factually and historically incorrect. Equality, in American history, meant equality of all humans, as opposed to a king and an aristocracy, it meant the political equality of all people, not the economic equality of a working class against a middle class or upper class.

The historical fight against slavery also had nothing to do with

Communism. The fight for gender equality and racial equality was based on the liberal ideals of gender-neutrality and race-blindness, and a belief that a person should be judged as an individual, and should not be politically racialized or gendered for no reason. It had no basis in Communism.

America was not perfect. There were early compromises and failures. The USA has always had some statist laws, which eroded freedom. Such as slavery, which amounted to the existence of a state race in the early USA. Or Prohibition, when alcohol was outlawed in the 1920s, as an attempt to make America become more of a Christian state. Or early American laws outlawing homosexuality, which were intended to impose or promote a state gender of cis-het (cisgender heterosexual).

There have been more recent failures also. FDR passed The New Deal in the 1930s in an attempt to turn America into a Communist state with a state economy, and his efforts were continued for decades, during the era of JFK and LBJ. After 9/11, Bush made an effort to turn the USA into a Fascist state defined by wars against the Muslim world, essentially to create a new Christian statist Crusade. Bush's and Obama's wars in the Middle East against nations that had little or nothing to do with 9/11 were the centerpiece of this folly.

Recently there has been a wave of laws from the Right to legislate race and gender, and the Left has countered with their own set of laws that seek to legislate race and gender.

But such errors were usually repaired. Such as by ending slavery in the United States, after the Civil War ended, in 1868. Or when Prohibition was repealed, by amending the United States Constitution, in 1933. Or when most anti-gay-sex laws were repealed at the state and federal level in the United States of America in the 1900s and early 2000s. Or when Reagan dismantled the Communist economic policies that had been passed under FDR, JFK, and LBJ, during the 1980s, and restored free market capitalism. As 9/11 faded from memory, so too did Bush's Fascism.

It is hoped that, as Americans forget the recent Culture Wars, the laws restricting freedom with respect to gender, and the laws that seek to legislate race and to racialize politics with respect to issues that have nothing inherently to do with race or racism at all, will also die, after those issues are forgotten. America might return to a race-blind and gender-neutral posture, which is the liberal ideal, although this has not yet happened.

The USA thrived, and prospered, and flourished, in the 1800s and 1900s. Why? Because just as the early American pioneers in the 1600s and 1700s had been able to survive in the frontier wilderness and carve out a prosperous life for themselves, so, too, every American citizen in the 1800s and 1900s was expected to own a set of skills that would enable them to survive in a harsh world on their own and yet still be able to live a happy life for themselves. And, mostly, they did.

A culture of rugged individualism led to a culture of innovation in the 1800s and 1900s. American geniuses invented things such as the light bulb, the mass-produced automobile, the airplane, and the nationwide train-based mass transit system. Things like this could only happen in America, because only in America were inventors free to try whatever they felt like, and run any experiment, without needing permission from the state. American inventions, technology, and industry are what drove progress around the world, not just in the USA.

More recently, the internet, and computer technology, evolved from the innovation of Silicon Valley. Why? How? Again, because there were technologists and businesspeople who were free to run experiments without needing to run to the state for approvals, so they were able to experiment, so they did experiment. No one needed a license to invent the personal computer or to invent the smartphone or to create content on the internet, people just did these things, in freedom, and then the state stepped in to tax and regulate them after the fact. This culture of freedom led to a culture of innovation, which drove progress, and created new wealth. Silicon Valley has often been called Liberal-tarian, which is one version of classical liberal.

Liberal democracy, and the liberal arts education, were

distinctly American ideas, although they held their genesis in the classical liberals of England.

But, over time, liberal democracy and the liberal arts education lost their original meaning, and gained a new meaning. The ideal of the liberal democracy faded.

Why? Because a new idea was imported to the USA from Europe, in the late 1800s and early 1900s, which replaced the idea of the liberal democracy. This new, European idea, was the conflict between the Communists and the Fascists. People came to believe that the choice that each person faced, and must make a choice among, was between Communism and Fascism, not between liberalism and tyranny, as had been believed by the founders of the United States of America.

The Communists infiltrated, and claimed, liberalism, so that the word liberal ceased to mean classical liberal, and instead came to mean socialist, which really means, Communist. The Communists used the word social liberal in contrast to the phrase classical liberal, but, over time, after having infiltrated the schools and universities, the Communist professors and teachers taught that social liberalism was liberalism, and that liberals meant social liberals, so the students, and the public, were not taught about classical liberalism, and they forgot.

Few people today know that the word liberal originally meant something more akin to today's libertarian, and not to modern liberal at all, although the term neo-liberal perhaps captures the meaning of original liberal.

The liberal arts education also changed its meaning, so that it meant a college or university education that was heavy in socialist ideas and Communist ideology, designed to convert and persuade young students to become Communists. It was mere abstract theory, with no practical value, and provided no career skills or money-making job training whatsoever such as would enable young students to become adults capable of making good money in a free-market capitalist economy. Nor did it teach critical thinking skills, because it did not want people to think, it only wanted people to obey Communism.

The colleges and universities stopped trying to teach people the skills to live as independent and self-reliant adults, in freedom, without being helped by the government. Instead, the new liberal arts education brainwashed people into dependence, and an inability to survive without state help, with the idea that everyone should be, and naturally already is, entirely dependent upon the government for their survival. And, having gone to such colleges and universities, where they were not taught the skills needed to live in freedom, a time came when many adults really could not survive on their own, and really were dependent upon state help.

Now, today, the ideas and ideals of classical liberalism have been revived, as Libertarianism and Objectivism. But, today, the Fascists are trying to do to Libertarianism precisely what the Communists did to liberalism. Invade it, conquer it, and change its meaning, so that Libertarian will mean Fascist.

If that happens, then everyone will forget what Libertarian really means. Just as, today, most people have forgotten what liberal used to really mean.

BUNCH OF CROOKS

Why does the government regulate an industry? To steal money from it. Why does the government regulate people's behavior? To steal money from them, and also to make them obey, to make them obedient. The politicians know this. They have no illusions. They're a bunch of crooks, they know exactly what they're doing. The people are sheep and the people are stupid, so the people don't know.

Less than one sixth of one percent of the US population are career politicians. 500,000 local, 20,000 state, and 500 federal career politicians, roughly, out of 300 million Americans, roughly. The politicians are a small group, a cabal, of crooks, who intend to rule, for one purpose, to steal money, which is what every crook's only goal ever is, and power is their tool to do so, and obedience is their weapon to achieve power. "Social conservative" means obey the Church, obey Christian politicians. "The Left" means obey the Democratic Party, obey the Marxists, obey Left culture. But it's a phony sham choice, and the ones offering it know this, they know it's poison as food and poison as antidote, they do it intentionally, the ones at the top on Left and Right are members of the same team with a personal rivalry between them, they know they're different factions of the same team.

The politicians have two goals: stealing money as taxes and regulatory fines, and creating obedience. Politicians create too many laws intentionally, because every time someone breaks a law, they have to pay a fine, which means that the politicians get to steal more money, so the politicians love to over-regulate and over-legislate, because they are crooks and they love theft, they love stealing money from the hardworking citizens, they want you to break their law, because they want more of your money. And then, if you have accepted the premise of the morality of the state, and you break a law, you feel guilty, which makes you feel humble and ashamed, and then you lose the will to take on the corrupt political establishment, because you blame yourself for breaking the law instead of blaming the politicians for passing a law that never needed to exist, and this creates obedience.

Take the examples of cannabis and gambling. It was illegal in order to create obedience, by regulating something that many people enjoy so much that they have to do it, to force as many people as possible to be subject to, and obey, as many laws as possible. But when people rebelled, the politicians shifted gears and made a strategic, intentional decision: say that they would legalize it, but they didn't legalize it (make it be free, give people the freedom to do it), instead they regulated it, by giving a small number of licenses to highly regulated cronies, which funnels people into a small number of sellers that the government can monitor and make sure they collect all the tax dollars and restrict supply to drive up price to maximize tax dollars. Politicians see the public as a source of revenue, their goal is to maximize tax dollars collected, intentionally and knowingly.

Cannabis and gambling were never truly free, instead, they went from being criminalized, as a feeder for jail for the prison system as a tool for obedience, to being regulated, as a feeder for the tax base as a tool for stealing money. Cannabis and gambling went out of the prison cell and into the tax collector's pocket. Real freedom would mean no regulations, and each person makes, sells, buys, and consumes, with no oversight, and no taxes collected.

Some people might then scream, in fear, because I propose repealing all safety laws and safety regulations in the USA. And the pretext of regulation is "safety," but the people who want that, in the context of cannabis and gambling, and prostitution, are the Christians who hate cannabis and hate gambling and hate sex work, so those votes funnel into regulation instead of criminalization, for gambling and cannabis, as a way to stick it to the people who want to gamble or who want to smoke cannabis, by making them jump through as many hoops as possible to get what they want, to make it more difficult for them, regulation is about torturing users while stealing their money.

Or, in the case of prostitutes, who are also called sex workers, it's about saying, as a pretext, that the product is so unsafe that no legal version should be made available, because the sex workers will be exploited or the clients will be led to sin or infidelity or whatever, in order to stick it to the users, by throwing them in jail, or threatening them with prison, just because you don't like them and you don't approve of the morality of what they do, because you are such a good virtuous pious Christian and instead of choosing your path they have chosen to have sex, which is your real reason and motive and purpose, not "safety," which is mere pretext, not reality.

For another, similar example, local city and town zoning regulations have absolutely nothing to do with safety, they are just a way for NIMBY local residents to stick it to the real estate developers whom they hate, because they get angry at increased traffic in their back yards, and then the politicians use the zoning laws, which often require some form of approval to build something new, to force the developers and businesses to pay them a campaign contribution, or a bribe under the table, to grease the wheels of the political approval process, in order to steal more money.

Everyone wants safety regulations for precisely the things that they hate, but they don't want the government to touch the things that they like or love. And everyone, or, at least, every smart person, who understands politics, and how politics works, knows this, and is well aware of this. When you play the game of laws, there is freedom, or else there is control, there is no middle ground.

It's as though the politicians view themselves as farmers and they view us as cash cows that they milk for money, but they also view us as wild dogs that roam around their farm, and they need to break us, and make us become obedient, and domesticate us, or else we'll get wild and cause trouble, and we might scare the cows. Or, God forbid, the dogs might attack the farmers and bite a farmer. The farmers' goal is to not let that happen, to prevent dog bites, while obtaining as much milk from the cows as possible, because that's a farmer's job, that's what being a farmer is. A politician is a politician. The government is the government. A farmer is a farmer.

Note that, while a wild dog loves freedom and hates being in a cage, and resents being whipped or kicked into obedience, and might simply give up and die in captivity, a cow doesn't want to be free, because a cow doesn't know the difference between freedom or its absence, a cow lacks any such concept of freedom, because it's just not smart enough to know, and so it doesn't know when it is not free and doesn't know the difference between being free or not being free, and, not knowing, it doesn't care. The cow can eat grass equally well on the farm or outside of the farm, so it doesn't care, and, yes, the farmer does take good care of the cows, and keeps the cows well fed, to maximize the milk output, so the farmer keeps the cows safe and fat, which makes the cows happy, at least until the time comes to slaughter the cows for beef.

You can't blame a cow for being a cow. A cow is a cow. A dog is a dog. And a farmer is a farmer. A thing is what it is. Everything is something.

It would be tough for Libertarians or Objectivists to do anything in this situation. We don't have the votes, because we don't have the voters, because so few people in the USA are Libertarians or Objectivists. People would have to get smarter, which may literally require human evolution.

But there is no place for Libertarians or Objectivists in either the Republican Party or the Democratic Party. Why? Because the Republican Party is actually the Christian Party, whose goal is to create an official state religion of Christianity. And the Democratic Party is really the Communist Party of America, whose goal is a Communist dictatorship, with all private property nationalized and seized and converted into publicly-owned state property.

Neither the Republicans or Democrats will ever admit to this, of course.

The Republicans say they will let people have religious freedom. And the Republicans say that they stand behind individual rights and the United States Constitution. The Republicans assert that, although they pass Christian laws, and they use the state to enforce those Christian laws, they are not Christian statists. They say they are fans of freedom and small government, and they do not desire a big Christian government, to impose Christian theology by force. They say they stand for freedom, and values, and morality, in a modern free society. They would say that their goal is not a return to the Christian states such as existed in Europe during the Middle Ages and Dark Ages. They would deny that they desire to destroy the separation of church and state, which is explicit in the Bill of Rights in the United States Constitution.

And the Democrats say they won't nationalize the entire economy and take total control for the government. The Democrats say that they stand behind democracy and won't create a Communist dictatorship. The Democrats call themselves democratic socialists, to emphasize their message that they are socialists, not Communists, by which they mean that they support democracy, not dictatorship. They say this, even though socialism means a government-owned economy, in which there is only public property and there is no private property, which will require an authoritarian regime, to seize all property from its private owners and give it to the state, and to use laws and state police to enforce the public ownership of all property and not allow anyone to ever hold or accumulate any private wealth.

Everyone knows that the GOP passes Christian laws, and the Dems pass Communist laws. But people are too cowardly or too unintelligent to make the leap of inference to understand that, yes, the goal of legislators in passing Christian laws is, in the end, state Christianity and a Christian state, and the goal of legislators who pass Communist laws is, as their final purpose, state Communism and a Communist state. Such laws, in the long-term grand scheme of things, can serve no other purpose than to climb towards the achievement of such goals, so it is perfectly rational, and logical, to infer those goals, and that purpose, and that meaning, from those laws.

Objectivists and Libertarians, even the Christian Libertarians, in general do not endorse any form of state religion, because state religion implies the existence of a state, and we oppose the state as such. So we do not fit comfortably in the Right. And we do not endorse or approve of any sort of government ownership or public property. So we are not members of the Left. Instead, we are outsiders, within both major parties in the two-party system in the USA.

If you listen to the rhetoric, on both sides, from both Left and Right, you can hear the truth, their true intentions, clearly, if you listen closely. And, quite frankly, their messaging is designed for the gullible and the naïve. And, if either the Republicans or the Democrats were to achieve their end goal of total political control, they would drop the act, in a hurry, having no more use for the mask that they wear. They would quite openly and honestly declare, for the GOP, that a Christian state is, and always was, their true end goal, or, for the Dems, that a Communist dictatorship in the USA was always their true hidden meaning.

In practice, the Left knows they cannot get a Communist dictatorship past the Right without triggering a full-scale Second Civil War in the USA. So, today, the Left is trying to create their Communist dictatorship gradually, slowly enough so that no one gets scared and fights back, instead of by a sudden bloody revolution.

The Left seeks to pass Communist law, after Communist law, after Communist law, to chip away at capitalism, to achieve Communism in small bits and pieces, so that no one notices what is happening, until, one day, so many Communist laws will have been passed that we will live in a Communist state, because everything in the economy will be fully regulated and all private wealth will have been taxed away.

But the Right is no different from the Left, at least not in terms of their goal of one-party rule. By means of a process of slowly passing a series of Christian laws, each one of which becomes more extreme than the last, the Right seeks the gradual, eventual creation of a Christian state, where Christianity is the official state religion, and defiance against the Church is outlawed. That would be a Christian state.

Why do the Left and Right do this slowly, by a process of laws, instead of swiftly, by revolution? To avoid scaring the voters, who might fight back if they foresaw the total loss of their freedom. And also because, if the Left staged a revolution, the Right would fight them, and, likewise, if the Right staged a revolution, the Left would fight them. So, instead of an open war, they fight the Culture Wars, waging their battles in American culture, and at the voting booth, and in state and federal legislatures, instead of on the battlefield.

What ultimately contains them both is the United States Constitution, which would force the armed forces of the USA to put down either revolt, of either the Far Left or the Far Right.

This is why recent Presidents, both Republican and Democrat, have worked tirelessly to erode the limits that the Constitution places upon the actions of the executive branch. It is because, in their dreams and fantasies, each Party longs to seize the White House, impose one-party rule, and eliminate the other Party.

Winning the Culture Wars is intended to be a first step to lay the groundwork for one-party rule, by either the Left or the Right. The content of the Left and of the Right differ sharply, but their strategy, and their ultimate goal, is the same: one-party rule. They both want one party to hold power, and to replace democracy with one-party rule. The only point with respect to which they differ is whether that one party of one-party rule should be the Democrats, or the Republicans.

What follows in this book is: First, a look at the Right, and how the Right seeks power. Second, an account of the Left, and how the Left obtains power. Third, a presentation of Libertarianism and Objectivism as a third path, that is neither Left nor Right, which could create or protect freedom. After that, a broader analysis of how it all fits together, in today's contemporary political paradigm.

THE RIGHT

Most Republicans are boring crusty rich old white guys. Their leaders and politicians mostly are, anyway. They are all of them old and elderly, in body or in spirit. Donald Trump's innovation was that he wasn't a boring crusty rich old white guy, instead, he was an exciting crusty rich old white guy. That's probably unique and can't be repeated.

The appeal of the GOP is that the GOP appeals mainly to those Christians who are stupid and ignorant, most of them over the age of 35 or older, and many of whom are downright elderly, who come for the promise of Christianity as a state religion. And the rich and powerful within the GOP are all of them boring crusty rich old white guys (other than one unique exception, Donald Trump, who is an exciting crusty rich old white guy). And boring crusty rich old white guys come to the GOP because it is a place that appreciates them and takes care of them.

Christianity is a missionary religion. The Christians believe that it is ethical and virtuous and gets them into Heaven to force other people to convert and obey, by force, by any means possible. It is only because the United States Constitution guaranteed certain inalienable basic human individual rights, including freedom of speech and the separation of church and state, that the USA is not a Christian nation. But the GOP, the Christian Party, desires a state religion. The goal of the Christian Republicans is nothing other than the forced conversion of all Americans to Christianity, and not merely to Christianity but to a very observant practice of Christianity.

The Republicans especially desire to force Christianity onto young people and the younger generations against their will, because the young tend to be less religious in their behaviors, and then young people sometimes become more religious as they grow older and become adults. However, the scope of the GOP's ambitions is not limited only to the young. They seek to forcibly convert all non-Christians, and all non-observant Christians, too, to be forced to obey Christian theology and perform observant Christian behaviors in their most extreme and strict religious form, with laws requiring all such behaviors, on penalty of imprisonment. Or, perhaps in the far future, on penalty of torture or death, much as existed in Europe during the Dark Ages.

If you think that a Christian state in the USA, with Christianity enforced by laws, is an idea of fiction, which could never really happen in America, because "America is a free country," so "it can't happen here," think again: the laws against the use of cannabis, and against recreational drug use, and laws prohibiting gambling, and laws criminalizing prostitution, were nothing other than laws designed to impose Christian morality onto the non-consenting or non-observant American public at large, to say nothing of Prohibition, the constitutional amendment against alcohol from the 1920s. So it has already been happening here, and it can happen here.

And many such laws, including the laws against prostitution, and the laws against recreational "hard" drug use, continue to be on the books, and enforced by jail time, to this day, throwing American citizens in jail because they did not choose to obey a code of Christian morality, in the Bible, with which they themselves do not agree, or which they did not choose to obey. Any smart person knows that any concern with "safety" as a pretext for all these laws, about drugs or whores or whatnot, is a sham. These laws are Christian laws, intended to promote theocracy and to destroy the separation of church and state and to dissolve religious freedom.

Let me briefly discuss abortion. The use of anti-abortion as an issue by the Right is not really about abortion at all. The abortion issue is not about abortion. The abortion issue is about Christianity. Yes, I said that, and I mean it. If it was only about the belief that abortion is murder, then the Right would be as angry about other forms of murder. Such as the meat-packing industry as the murder of animals, or the murder of poor Blacks and Latinos in urban inner city poverty, or the murder of people from capital punishment in cases where guilt is never clearly proven, or to simply get angry whenever any murder of a human being is reported by the press.

We see none of this. So a wise person would look behind the rhetoric of murder to find the real truth about anti-abortion laws. The real motive of anti-abortion laws is that Christian theology says that the soul attaches to the body at conception, and also says that, if the baby dies before the baby is baptized, then the baby's soul goes to Hell. The anti-abortion laws are designed to implement this Christian theology in a Christian state by forcing women not to have abortions.

Forcing women not to have abortions has only one motive: to impose Christian theology onto women against their will. These women are often unwed mothers or women who did not observe Christian ethics in their sexual behaviors, so the Right particularly enjoys punishing these women, whom they regard as sinners, by forcing them to obey the Christian Church.

The interesting thing about the abortion issue, and what makes it unique, is that you can make a plausible argument, from a secular non-Christian point of view, that abortion is murder, if the fetus is a human life. So, by making abortion a central issue, the Christian Right can get large numbers of moderate and independent voters to support anti-abortion. This energy that gets poured into the anti-abortion movement is ultimately directed towards the broader social movement to create a Christian state. And so the Christian statists pull a scam or con on the American people with the abortion issue, by tricking them into thinking that it is about abortion, when it is really about the Christian state. The passage of anti-abortion laws has become a symbol of the passage of Christian law in general.

"Religious freedom" is the freedom to not be a Christian in America, "religious freedom" is not the freedom to pass Christian laws, which is how the Republicans have twisted and wrongly defined that word. The "freedom" to force your religion onto non-consenting others against their will is not freedom. And there are many other things far more dangerous, and less safe, than hard drugs or cannabis or prostitutes, such as alcohol consumption, or owning a gun, or, perhaps, even running your own small business that you invested all your money into, which are legal, and which the Christian zealots and Christian prudes love, and never say should be regulated in the same way that they want to regulate what they regard as "sin" crimes under a pretext of safety.

The only people in the GOP other than Christians are, by and large, Orthodox Jews and Conservative Jews, and, perhaps, Objectivists and Libertarians.

The Orthodox Jews and Conservative Jews believe that, if Christianity becomes the state religion, then there will be no separation of church and state any longer, and they think that, if this happens, they will be able to declare Judaism as an official religion within their own small and insular Jewish communities, and to enforce Judaism and Jewish law within their communities by force of law, by means of the legal system of the government.

The Objectivists and Libertarians are simply very confused, and are taken in by the GOP's promise of economic freedom and virtues and values and morality, and fail to see that the GOP's morality is distinctly Christian morality, and the GOP's economic freedom is rooted in nothing more than the "Protestant work ethic," that people who get married, have kids, don't drink, and work hard, and don't make trouble and don't make waves, often get rich and get promoted at work or become middle-class, and such people tend to be Christian, so the Christians love capitalism, for as long as capitalism suits Christianity (and not for one moment longer). If Christianity becomes a state religion, then all non-Christians will be forced to convert, by the Christian government, and even those who do not convert will be forced to obey laws that legislate Christian morality, and we Objectivists, too, will be subjected to this, if it happens, and the GOP's only purpose is to cause this to happen.

But let us also not forget the moderate Republicans: There are, of course, moderate Republican voters who do not desire to see the total destruction of the constitutional separation of church and state and the formation of a Christian state, and, of course, the GOP is perfectly happy to exploit the votes of these moderate Republicans in order to help elect Republican politicians, who are dedicated to the GOP's agenda of creating a Christian theocratic state.

You might ask: why do the Christian statists desire the formation of a Christian state? The Christians view themselves as weak, and the Christians view themselves as sinful, so the Christians desire a strong, powerful government to force them to obey Christian theology, because they are not strong enough to obey Christian theology on their own, of their own free will. The Christians do not care about the cost to society as loss of freedom, so long as they get what they want. The Christians are essentially willing to do a deal with the Devil in order to be forced to walk the path of God.

The Republicans have cast themselves as the party of tradition. But, because of the clauses in the Bill of Rights regarding the separation of church and state in the United States Constitution, which forbids the establishment of any official state religion, there has never actually been an official Christian state in the USA, ever, in American history. So what the GOP really desires is actually radical and new.

(Note that I do not count whatever governments existed in North America prior to 1776, before the formation of the USA as a nation. Witch hunts, for example, were an early form of Christian statism in the USA, as the Communists so cleverly knew when they accused the McCarthy Anti-Communists of a witch hunt.)

However, in Europe, there is a long history of Christian states. So, when the GOP speaks of tradition, the tradition to which they truly refer is European tradition during the Dark Ages and Middle Ages, it is no tradition that ever existed in the history of America.

Perhaps what they think that they mean is that in older eras people were more religious and more religiously observant than they are today in modern society, and that is the tradition to which they refer, but the quality of being religious, as such, is a private matter, that does not tie directly to politics; the GOP, as the Christian Party, is focused not upon causing people to become more religious, but is instead focused with singular intensity upon the creation of a Christian state, with Christian laws that legislate Christian morality, perhaps for the purpose of promoting religion, or, perhaps, merely for the purpose of obtaining power.

THE LEFT

We have seen the appeal of the GOP. What, then, is the appeal of the Democrats?

Democrats traffic in victimhood and outrage, and Democrats sacrifice the healthy to save the sick.

When something bad happens, when an injustice happens, people get angry, and people want to blame someone or something, and then people want somebody to take action, and to do something to make sure it never happens again, and to punish the cause that they blame for it. People when they feel anger do not think, or reason, or use logic, instead, they are inflamed by emotion, and they become unable to think or reason again until their anger has cooled off, usually after they feel that somebody took action and did something to punish someone or to make sure it never happens again. Democrats feed off of that, Democrats feed off of anger.

For example, a mass shooting by a deranged lone gunman happens. People feel anger, and they feel sympathy for the victims, and they want this to never happen again. They do not ask, using reason and logic, whether it is humanly possible to prevent every potential lone gunmen, even those with no red flags or forewarnings, to ever get a gun and shoot someone, or whether it is possible to cure every person's mental health and make every human being be perfectly sane. They do not ask using reason and logic, because they feel anger, and can't use reason and logic until their anger passes.

So Democrats offer gun control, not because any rational logical person thinks it will work, or that it is feasible to actually confiscate all the guns from everyone given enforcement issues and the fact that most gun-owning Americans will simply refuse to comply with gun control laws because either they're criminals or they know they have a right to bear arms for self-defense. And not because anyone really thinks it's possible to cure any and every insanity and mental health disorders to prevent any person who will ever have access to a gun to ever become an untreated psycho nutjob who wants to kill innocent people at random, such that in a nation of over one hundred million adults not one crazy lunatic ever gets his hands on a gun, ever. Or what system could actually achieve that likelihood, given the probability math with the numbers involved. But because people are angry, and they want someone to do something.

For other examples, say that you are openly gay, and someone insults you with a homophobic insult. You feel anger, and you want justice and revenge, and you want someone to do something, so that the bigot is punished and it never happens again. You don't use reason and logic to ask if this is possible or how this could actually be done, that thought-control and mind-police would literally have to control all speech and all thought to ban any anti-gay idea or anti-gay speech from ever existing anywhere, and you don't use reason and logic to ask what that would do to freedom, or what sort of dictatorship and secret police and loss of civil liberties is necessary to achieve that. You don't care, because you're angry and you want results.

Say that you are poor and a loved one dies, and you blame the hospital and your lack of money that you couldn't afford to send them to a better hospital. You feel you have been wronged, and you blame capitalism and the healthcare system, and you're angry, and you want someone to do something, to punish the villain and prevent the injustice from ever happening again. And you do not use reason and logic to ask how much the better hospital would have cost, and, because you could not pay that price, who could have paid, and, if the answer is the rich, how they could have paid, and, if the answer is for government to tax the rich to fund healthcare, the next question is do all the rich have enough money to pay for everyone like you and all the poor people to have everything nicer and better that the rich and middle class have, given the objective prices of costs and benefits involved.

And the economic data says no, there isn't enough money in the world to pay for nice great high-quality things for everyone, mostly there's only enough money for each person to pay for what they have for themselves. But you're angry, and you don't want to hear it, you just want free healthcare, you demand free healthcare, and you don't care that the taxpayers literally can't afford to pay for it and it's not humanly possible to provide free high-quality healthcare for everyone if the buyers don't make enough money to pay the costs of the sellers in delivering that healthcare.

You scream, angrily, that it is totally unacceptable for even one person to die due to poverty, or else capitalism must be destroyed. Even though, sometimes, oftentimes, every day in fact, people do die, and humans are mortal, and there isn't a magic spell that the government can cast so that no one ever dies and everything is perfectly safe from deadly risk and everyone lives forever.

Yet, nonetheless, most often, if someone's loved one or friend or family members die, they get angry, and demand that government do something to punish the culprits and make sure it never happens again. But this anger is totally illogical, because humans are animals, human beings are a type of animal, and animals are mortal beings in the physical world, who face mortal risk every day, and animals have accidents or get sick or get attacked or fail to find food to eat or get wounded and fail to find a way to heal, and, yes, then, they die. And there's nothing the government can do about that by passing a law or switching from capitalism to socialism, even though anger always wants to blame someone and to punish someone and for someone to do something so that it can't happen to someone else ever again.

And this is simply the nature of anger. And it is also the nature of anger to destroy logic and reason until such time as anger passes and the emotional state returns to being calm and cool and collected and even-tempered, without anxiety or panic or hatred or rage.

Say, for my final example, that your brother was taken in by a financial fraud, a Ponzi scheme or con game or was sold a defective item at a high price by a fraudulent seller who disappears the next day, or he put his money in a bank that turns out to be crooked and collapses and his money vanishes.

You're angry, you feel anger, your brother was the victim of an injustice, you want someone to do something about it, you want to punish whom you blame and pass laws so that it will never happen again. You don't ask, using cool, calm, emotionless reason and logic, how and under what conditions this could actually never happen to anyone again, that you would need to eliminate human stupidity and human ignorance so there are no suckers, or eliminate the existence of evil from human nature and render it impossible to ever choose evil or wrong so that criminals and con men will never exist again, neither of which can be done, because humans are humans, and human nature is what it is, and this is not a perfect world, and we humans control our own choices but we cannot alter human nature itself, perhaps other than through genetic engineering, and maybe even that wouldn't eliminate evil or stupid.

But you don't want to hear it, you just want justice, and the Democrats say, let us regulate the economy, and then we won't let there be more frauds like this, and we will punish every crook in business, and this will never happen again.

And then, if and when it does happen again, the Democrats will say it's because the voters didn't give us enough power as regulators to stop all of it, we needed total control of everything in order for our system to work, and the solution is to give the Democrats more power, not to blame the Democrats for having failed.

It's as Ayn Rand wrote in Atlas Shrugged (paraphrased): "The Marxists fail, but then, instead of conceding that they failed, they say that we were not noble enough to spill all the blood that their system required in order to succeed."

The only imaginable conceivable way that all financial fraud and economic crime and unethical economic behavior and economic collapse and recession, all the injustice and evil and outrage and victimhood that causes the anger, could be eliminated, would be to put the entire economy, down to every last detail, out of the hands of the public or any private individual, and put the entire economy, in every detail, completely under the control of regulators who are perfect robots. Robots devoid of human emotions and human faults and human weakness and human fallibility and human motivations and human psychology and human selfishness, who would be perfectly selfless and wise and powerful and knowledgeable. Robots who, for no reason other than having been programmed to do so, would manage everything and make every economic decision for everyone on everyone's behalf for everyone's benefit in a perfect way.

Because then the stupidity and gullibility and ignorance of individuals, of us humans, would no longer render them (in other words, us) vulnerable to victimization by sleazy crooks.

But such perfect robots do not exist, and the Dems pretend that the Democratic politicians and regulators are these perfect robots. And it is fake, it's a con, a scam, a mask, they are just dirty stinking stupid ignorant humans pretending to be perfect selfless robots, so that we will trust them to run the economy for our benefit for the purpose that no financial frauds or economic crimes or stupid risks or economic collapses will ever happen again. And it's an impossible goal, and their solution is impossible, there is no such thing as a perfect regulator, the regulator robots don't exist and the regulator humans are neither selfless nor intelligent nor all-knowing nor all-powerful, instead, they are humans with human motivations and human psychology and human limits and human self-interest.

I leave for another day the debate I could have, as an Objectivist, about what "selfless" or "selfish" really means in this context, and whether it is good to be selfless and evil to be selfish, or not, according to the philosophy of Objectivism. And also, why on earth anyone would realistically expect that the regulators would be selfless and special and intelligent and knowledgeable, and be perfect experts and servants of humanity, if all other humans are not, if they and we are all of us human, and this is all of it coming from our human nature. As an Objectivist, I think that it is good to be selfish, and that human nature is naturally selfish. Much of the evils of Communism arise because, by trying to force us to be selfless, the Communist government is trying to force us to defy our own nature as humans.

Democrats, for every outrage, for every injustice, have one solution: give more power to the Democrats to regulate, and give more money to the Democrats to spend as taxes taken from the rich, and if you give enough money and power to the Democrats, they will punish everyone and prevent everything. And they're a bunch of crooks, and they've figured out the perfect psychology to get everyone who is a victim of any injustice to be motivated by their anger to give as much money and power as they possibly can to the Democrats. The Democrats just lie and say they can do things they cannot do, like turn this world into a perfect world where every crook is punished and nothing extremely bad ever happens because nothing evil is ever allowed to happen.

They promise a world with perfect safety where everything is given to everyone for free, if you would just give them enough money and power, if you would just give them all the money and all the power, and it's a lie. The metaphysical nature of the physical world and human life and the very physics and chemistry of motion dictates that there is no such thing as perfect safety, there is no perfectly safe workplace, no perfectly safe school, and so on, and everything can't be free, the money to pay to create all the stuff to give away does not exist, all the money in the world literally is not enough money to pay for it mathematically and economically.

It's a lie, to collapse freedom into a socialist dictatorship, and by the time it happens, the Democrats control education and control the media, so things go to the point where the government controls what people are taught, what people say, what people think, and can pitch any state lie that they want, and censor all dissent, like any Communist Party, and by then it's too late for the people to wake up from their anger and realize it was all a lie and what they were promised wasn't possible and to prevent the

Communists from taking over, and then there's no freedom, just a Communist state dictatorship.

Everyone knows that socialists are idealists and that it never works in practice, and people don't understand, then, why the socialists are socialists when everyone tells them it's an impossible ideal that will never work. And that explains why. It would be a perfect world, in which there was no racism and no gender-discrimination and everyone had enough money to buy everything they wanted and everyone could afford a perfect great version of their every need.

But reason and logic say this isn't possible, it is only anger that clouds the judgment which makes people demand this, in anger, and the Democrats, like a crooked used car salesman, sell a faulty product to suckers, sell the cure for everyone's anger, and then, like a crooked used car salesman, steals the sucker's money and power, just by putting a great paint job on a defective car that was really always a piece of crap, and giving the sucker crap in return for the sucker's money and power. The more power you give to the Democrats, the less you keep for yourself. The more power the people concede to their government, the less there actually exists real power for the people.

The voters always want the Democrats to "do something" to cure every outrage and solve every injustice, the only problem is that, when it comes right down to it, when it's time to take action, no one actually knows what in the world to actually do, no one has a real plan to solve the problem, so they talk and talk and never find a solution, and the voters know it, and it angers and frustrates them, so they vote out the last batch of crooks and vote in the next bunch of crooks, who have sold them on some new plan or new idea, and then nothing happens again, and the reason for this, is that there really isn't anything that anyone can do to solve most of these problems, most of these problems arise from the metaphysical nature of reality, and it's outside the scope of human control to "solve" this, to prevent these problems from ever happening again, but people get angry and demand that someone do something, and so the Dems get their votes.

There are, of course, moderate Democrats, who do not desire the creation of a Communist state in the USA, and who are willing to walk a short way down the path towards Communism, but who do not want to go all the way down that path, and who do not want to reach the total Communism at the end of that path. And, of course, the Democratic Party is more than happy to exploit the votes of these moderate Democrats, in order to elect Democratic politicians, who are fully intent upon the creation of a Communist state. The moderate Democrats should join the Libertarians, but they are not smart enough to do so, so they have no place else to go, other than the Democratic Party, and they know that they have no place else to go, so they are stuck being Democrats, even though they are not Communists.

RACE AND GENDER

Other than the Christians, there is one other type of Republican, and, other than the victims of injustice and those in anger and outrage, one other type of Democrat, and, ironically, they are the same type, the person for whom everything is race or everything is gender or everything is race and gender.

This type of Republican desires a state race (white, especially white of European descent) or a state nationality (white American) or a state culture (white Christian American) to be imposed by force onto all Americans, with the state race in control of the state, and the state in control of everyone else, and all others either marginalized or oppressed or deported or simply eliminated by ending their life.

The equal but opposite type of Democrat sees everything as race and thinks that everything is race, everything that exists explicitly is a subtext or pretext for an implicit racial meaning, and the hidden meaning of everything is racism and racial bias, there is no such thing as an honest explicit literal meaning that doesn't have something to do with racism, ever, anywhere, so they desire a government that will impose a perfect balance of racial equality and equity and diversity and inclusion onto everyone by force, so that, for any random sample set of a group of Americans, they will have a perfectly balanced racial composition, and, if they don't, one will be given to them by force, by state laws.

Or, for gender, the GOP desires a state gender, cisgender, or, in its most extreme form, the GOP desires a favored state gender of cis-het (cisgender hetero) male, to be imposed onto all by force, with laws that state that only cisgender is true gender, or that only cis-het is true gender. Such laws would forcibly convert the

Communists to the traditional Christian belief that only cis-het gender is real gender, and that marriage is between a man and a woman, etc.

And the Dems desire a state gender, queer or transgender or LGBTQ, or a state culture, trans culture and queer culture and LGBTQ culture, to be imposed onto all by force, with laws that state that transgender and cisgender are equally real true gender. Such laws would forcibly convert the Christians to Communism, by forcing the Christians to disobey their own Christian theology, which states that all sexuality is a sin and all gender-fluidity is a sin, and forcing the Christians to be accepting of queer and trans and LGBTQ against their will.

Christian religious freedom does violate the rights of trans and queer and gay people to be free from hatred and from discrimination. However, the reverse is also true: laws that mandate equality for queer and LGBTQ people, in people's private daily lives, does violate the rights of Christians to practice their religion according to their theology's teachings and to obey their own moral conscience, which tells them that they feel that queer is wrong and evil.

Christian theology does say that queer and trans and gay and LGBTQ are evil, because all of these things arise from sex and sexuality. Being gay is about what sex you are attracted to, while being trans is about what sex you self-define as, so it all has to do with sex. And Christian theology says that sex is a sin.

So, if there is religious freedom, if Christians are free to practice Christianity, then the Christians will have the right to reject and discriminate against LGBTQs.

Or, if there are laws that force everyone to treat all LGBTQs with respect and dignity, then that will destroy religious freedom, because the Christians will not have the ability to act out and express their Christian attitudes towards sex.

It's an either/or. You cannot have it both ways.

The gays, queers, trans people, and LGBTQs, complain bitterly that Christian freedom should not mean that the Christians have the right to hate them and discriminate against them.

But the LGBTQs are not the ones who get to decide what Christian theology says. The Christians get to decide that. And the Christians have decided that Christianity hates queers. So, yes, religious freedom, for Christians, would require the freedom to be anti-LGBTQ.

However, LGBTQs, to be able to live happy lives, also require freedom. Just as the Christians, not the LGTBQs, are the ones who get to decide what Christian theology says about LGBTQ, so, too, the Christians are not the ones who get to decide if being gay or trans is real, instead, it is the gays and the trans who are the ones who get to decide if being gay and trans is real. The queers decide how to practice queer identity, and how live an authentic LGBTQ life, the Christians have no right to decide that for the queers. The Christians can decide, for the Christians, whether the Christians believe that LGBTQ is real. But the LGBTQs are are the ones who get to decide, for the LGBTQs, whether they are LGBTQs, and, if so, how to live an LGBTQ life.

So it seems that a war between Left and Right is inevitable. Is it the Christians who will be free? And the queers who will be enslaved? Or is it the queers who will be free? And the Christians who will have their rights deprived? Because it seems like there is no system where all sides could have freedom.

But there is such a system. A system where everyone enjoys absolute and total freedom, and is able to be alive, and practice their identity, freely, at will.

It is Libertarianism and Objectivism.

The Libertarian and Objectivist position, in contrast, is to get the government out of the business of legislating race and legislating gender at all, and let each individual do whatever they want for themselves. There should be no state race, and there should be no state gender, ever, for any reason, under any circumstances.

Cis-het should not be the official state gender. Queer and LGBTQ should not be the official state gender. There should be no official state gender at all. And there should be no laws attempting to legislate gender or attempting to create an official state gender.

That solves the problem. That will create freedom for everyone, Christian and LGBTQ queer.

The fact that there should be no official state race is probably more clear to more people. But the war over "Woke" culture is a ploy that is similar to gender, in the sense that it is designed to make people feel that war is inevitable, so that they give up on peace.

The Left says that the Right is racist against Blacks. And then the Right says that the Left is racist against whites. I am willing to agree with the statement that a person must be able to be free from racism, in general, in order to be able to live a happy life. This is true for Blacks and would also be true for members of any and every race.

Is the Left legitimate when they say that all members of the Right are racist? Is the Right racist, as a factual question? Is it valid for the Right to accuse the Left of making everything be about race, which fans the flames of racism? Does the history of racism, and slavery, and racial segregation, and racial inequality, in American history, play a role in what job politics has to perform today? Are we, people alive today, morally responsible for what our ancestors did, or had done to them, 200 years ago? Is an individual ever responsible for the actions of their race, and is a race ever responsible for the actions of one individual? Should, or can, the political process work to achieve racial equality, diversity, equity and inclusion?

The real answer is that there is no need to answer any of these questions, or, at least, there is no need for an official state answer, embodied in laws, to any of these questions. This is the answer: there should be no state race. Ever. There should be no laws that legislate race. In any way. Ever. Once you accept that premise, then the answers to all of the above questions become private, subjective matters of personal opinion. They might influence your private decisions, but they hold no political significance.

Ultimately, this means that a Libertarian government would be race-blind and gender-neutral. Now, some Dems would assert that race-blind means white, and gender-neutral means cis-het (cisgender hetero) male, because, they say, it is only for white people that it is possible for race to not be an issue, race is always an issue automatically for every Black person, and gender is always an issue for every woman, it is only for cis-het men that gender could be a non-issue.

But these people are simply ignorant of what the words "race-blind" and "gender-neutral" mean, in this context, as I use them, and so, lacking the knowledge or intelligence to know what the words mean, they default to the words they know, and so they assume that race-blind means white and gender-neutral means cis male, but words have meanings, those meanings exist objectively, and that is not, in fact, what those words mean. Race-blind means that you do not make decisions or take actions based upon race, at all, for any race. Gender-neutral means that you treat any and all genders in exactly the same way, and you take no positions as to the validity or reality of any gender, you do nothing based upon gender in any way. Given the real meanings of words, I stand by my statements.

Note, by the way, that I believe that cisgender and transgender are both real true equally valid genders, and in fact I know that this is true. However, the issue isn't what I believe. The issue here is what the government should do. And I believe, in fact I know, that the government should be gender-neutral and should let everyone believe, say, and do, whatever the fuck they want.

To be precise, the form of government in which there is an official state race is properly called Fascism, and, yes, Fascism is evil, and, no, Libertarians are not Fascists. A state with an official state gender of cis-het, or an official state race of white, would be either a Christian State or a white-of-European-descent Fascist State. A state which had an official state race in the form of an official state preference for Blacks, or an official state preference for diversity among all races, would be a type of Left-Fascist state, while also being a Communist state. An official state preference for queers and LGBTQs would be a Communist State, but it would also be a form of a religious state, in the sense that it would have legislated religion by banning the practice of Christian religion, in one aspect very important to the Christians, namely, their attitudes towards sex and gender.

It is textbook Libertarianism that we Libertarians reject all forms of Communism, Fascism, Christian statism, and state race, and state religion, and state gender, in all forms. We reject state race, and we reject state religion, because we reject the state, as such.

Every area where the government is forced to take a position on race or gender, such as the gender of public restrooms in public schools, or the race of college and university admissions, should not exist, because the government should not be owning and operating public schools to begin with, and the government should not be legislating university admissions either. Education is not the job of the government. And there should be no public schools, only private schools.

What private schools do is not the problem of the government and does not require any role for the state. And, if the government adhered closely to only its proper role and was limited to only its proper scope, then the government would have no situations where it had to pass laws that legislate race or that legislate gender, ever.

Obviously, the government must pass laws which outlaw the existence of slavery, and such laws are valid and just. However, this is not a case which requires race to be legislated, because slavery should be outlawed for all races. It should be a crime to enslave someone regardless of what their race happens to be. So it is possible for the government to ban and outlaw slavery, without having to specify any particular race.

Also note, by the way, that it should never be legal for someone to consent to become a slave or to consent themselves into slavery, as some crazy Libertarians believe, because the basis of all valid and just laws is the protection of individual rights, the only valid purpose of laws is to protect or enforce rights, and slavery is a fundamental violation of human rights, therefore there can be no legal basis to ever enforce slavery, even if a person consented to become a slave or tried to sell themselves into slavery, so slavery can never be legal, and whether it was initially chosen or consented to is not relevant to any legal or political analysis.

WHAT IS THE CULTURE WARS?

Like Christianity, Communism, too, is a missionary religion, or, if you are not willing to define Communism as a religion, you must at least concede that Communism is a missionary ideology. Just as the goal of true Christians is world Christianity and a global Christian state, the goal of all Communists is world Communism and a global Communist state. The Communist Party of America, the Democratic Party, desires the forced conversion of all Americans to Communism, with Communism taught in all public schools and public universities, and then enforced by laws that require all to obey the economic and ideological edicts of the Communist regime.

The Christians, naturally, do not want to be forcibly converted to Communism, much as the Communists do not want to be forcibly converted to Christianity, hence the "Culture Wars" today in the United States of America.

What is the Culture Wars? The Christians and the Communists are fighting a war against each other, but it is a war fought in culture, in the media, in education, in journalism, in values and beliefs, in philosophy, etc. Each side is not ready, or is not willing, to yet take up arms and fight the other in open armed combat, so they fight in culture, in the media, instead.

The Christians seek to control our culture, for example by passing laws to ban drag shows, or ban gay books from school libraries, or prevent trans people from choosing which restrooms to use, or ban abortions, in order to forcibly convert the

Communists to Christianity.

Meanwhile, the Communists seek to take control of the culture, for example by cancel culture, which stages protests against any Right-wing media person who seeks to give a lecture in a college or university, and which labels all Right-wing thought as mere disinformation, or by Woke culture, which labels all members of the Right as racists, and which asserts that capitalism is racist, without any basis in fact or logic to justify that assertion, in order to forcibly convert the Christians to Communism.

Both sides employ an identical agenda: label the opponent as offensive, censor them in the name of censoring offensive content, and then pass laws to enact and enforce that censorship. The goal of such censorship is to destroy the opponent's voice within the culture, thereby obtaining the opportunity to win the Culture Wars by means of turning it into a one-sided debate.

The result is a condition of extreme animosity and disrespect, where the Left and the Right hate and disrespect each other, do not view each other as human beings, does not treat the other side with respect, and seeks to villify and demonize the other side, and then creates an echo chamber on their internet and social media networks, to maximize the degree to which they are extreme and outrageous.

In their echo chamber, there is no sane person to tell them to stop acting like a child throwing a tantrum, and to instead behave like a civil, respectful adult.

The Left and the Right are mirror images of each other in their gameplan for how to fight the Culture Wars. The content is different, but the tactics are the same.

Both sides wants a culture, a media, an education system, an arts and entertainment, a news and journalism, which will brainwash everyone to join their side and hate the other side. Freedom, and critical thinking skills, and the ability to question authority, are their greatest enemies.

Ironically, each side fails because the other side is using precisely the same strategy, so what we end up with is a culture where roughly half is Christian and half is Communist, and, because neither side has a majority, neither side has the power to win the war enough to cause a majority to form for itself.

But this is not intended to be a futile or endless war, by either side. Each side has a goal. And it is the same strategy. They are trying to convert as many people to their side, by means of cultural influence and cultural persuasion, as possible, to one day gain a majority among voters, to achieve one-party rule. At which point that one party, whichever wins, will outlaw and abolish the other party.

The GOP and Dems both desire one-party rule, they would both love to destroy democracy and replace it with themselves as rulers. They both want one-party rule, but they differ only with respect to which party they think should be the one.

Why fight a war in culture, instead of an open armed conflict? Because that would require a Second Civil War, and neither side is sure whether they would win or lose such a war, so they want to win the war of culture, and win the war of ideas, to gain a numbers advantage.

Trust me, if one side believed that they could win a Second Civil War, then they would fight one. But the Left and the Right both do not know that they would win such a war, whether it would become North vs. South again, or how the moderates and independents would go. And many of the people on the Left and Right have a bark that is far worse than their bite, and they act mean and nasty on the internet, but they would shit their pants in fear if they had to fight an actual war. They would rather fight in the Culture Wars first, and then leave the actual combat for a later time, when they feel they have already won. As Sun Tzu said in The Art of War, "do not fight the battle until you have already won it."

So they bide their time, and fight the war in culture, waiting to gain a decisive advantage, and then win.

PARTY LOYALTY

It is worth discussing the politicization of science as an example of how political parties arbitrarily and subjectively assign political meanings to neutral objects in an insane way as a test of party loyalty to see if you will obey the insanity of your political party in the interests of loyalty to them, to see if you will go along with their crazy insane arbitrary and subjective meanings instead of what exists as things in objective reality, as a test of your party loyalty. The loyalty test is testing your obedience, and conditions you to always see everything, even science, from a partisan point of view, and to lose all concepts of objective or neutral or unbiased truth. Let me point to two examples: Covid vaccines, and climate change.

Were, and are, the Covid vaccines safe and effective? They might be. Time will tell. We shall see. But the Dems decided that the vaccines are safe, the Democrats decided that the Covid vaccines are definitely safe and there is no possibility whatsoever that they can have any short-term or long-term side effects whatsoever, therefore everyone had to agree and obey and be forced to be vaccinated against their will, and all dissent and debate and criticism had to be rejected, and stigmatized, as mere "disinformation," because only the Democratic Party can have knowledge, and, if the Democratic Party says something, then that must be God's own truth.

But then, because the Dems had decided that the vaccines are safe, the GOP then had to say the vaccines are unsafe, and refuse to take them, to defy and disagree and criticize and reject the Dems, not because of the science, but in order to make a political statement, a statement of defiance against the Democrats. The

Dems assigned the meaning of loyalty to the Democratic Party to taking the vaccine, and the GOP assigned the meaning of loyalty to the GOP by rejecting the vaccine, and, from an objective point of view, it's insane, the Covid vaccines, and their safety and effectiveness, were an issue of science, not politics. The Covid vaccines are safe, or else they aren't, and what is actually true would be true whether you were a Dem or a GOP or lived on a desert island where there is no politics. Science is objective, but a set of arbitrary political meanings were assigned to certain scientific positions, not because of the science, but to test loyalty and foster obedience.

A similar example is climate change. Is climate change real? It might be. Is it caused by humans and air pollution? It might be caused by humans and air pollution. But, if it is, then the oil and gas industry is partly to blame. The oil and gas industry funds the pro-business lobby and funds the GOP and skews Republican. So the Dems assigned being anti-business and being anti-oil and gas and being anti-GOP to believing that climate change is real. This then forced the GOP, in conjunction, perhaps, with the efforts of the oil and gas lobby, to assign the meaning of being pro-GOP and being a Republican to the position that climate change isn't real or isn't human-caused, to being a climate skeptic or a climate denier. The science of climate change is neutral and objective and unbiased, because science itself, real science, is neutral and objective and unbiased, and, if reason and logic and science were the only things in play, there is no logical reason why a Republican pro-business person couldn't believe that climate change is real, if they looked at the science and thought that is what it showed, and there is equally no reason why an anti-business Democrat couldn't be a climate skeptic or climate denier, if they looked at the objective science and thought, honestly, that it showed that climate change isn't really real.

But the Dems and GOP have assigned political meanings in an arbitrary and subjective way to what would otherwise have been apolitical neutral unbiased objective facts, and the game is used in exactly the same way by both parties, to look for people who don't obey, who think independently about the science for themselves, to look for people who are disloyal, who don't march in lockstep with everything the party does, who don't obey the party bosses and just go along with the party's insanity.

THE LIBERTARIANS AND OBJECTIVISTS

What is the alternative? Libertarianism and Objectivism. Libertarianism is not precisely the same thing as Objectivism, but, for purposes of the analysis in this book, they mean one thing. So:

No forcible conversion to other people's beliefs that you do not voluntarily choose to follow. No obedience to the state. Each person has the freedom to choose what they believe, as an individual, and to choose how they practice their beliefs, as an individual.

No jail or prison for victimless or non-violent crime.

Completely legalize and de-regulate, with no safety regulations, no licenses, and no taxes collected, all gambling, cannabis, other recreational drugs, and prostitution.

No state religion. No missionary Christianity imposed by force. No laws that legislate morality. No religious statism, and no religious state. No Christian state. No official state religion.

No state economy. No economic statism. No regulations. No taxes. No state theft. No occupational licenses. No state-granted licenses of any kind. Pure unregulated capitalism.

No state race. No state gender.

No public education. No state brainwashing. No state media, no government propaganda. No laws that censor or stifle freedom of speech. No classified information. No libel or slander or defamation laws. No non-disclosure agreements.

No censoring of profanity on television. No one forces you to watch the tv shows with foul language, and you have no right to force other people to talk how you want.

No anti-speech discrimination laws. People can say whatever they want, and if you don't like it, don't listen, or walk away from them and go somewhere else. You don't have the right to control them or boss them around just because you don't like what they say and you feel it's evil and wrong. The fact that someone said something that hurt your feelings or gave you a sense of horror and outrage is not a valid justification to pass a new law.

People can say what they want, think what they want, and do what they want, according to their own freedom, by their choice. And you can't stop them, unless they use violence against you, and then you can defend yourself with violence for self-defense only.

Probably no government at all, and no politicians, therefore no theft, no obedience, no one to steal your money and power.

Or, absent that, a very small state, only to administer police to stop rape and murder and violent assault and armed robbery only, an army to block foreign invaders, and the courts, and courts only for the purpose of settling disputes which would otherwise be guaranteed to erupt into bloodshed with someone being wrongfully attacked in anger.

Instead of state Christianity and a Christian state, or state Communism and a Communist state, I would prefer freedom, quite frankly, if it's all the same to you, if that's okay.

Let me briefly extol the virtues of democracy. A democracy is a plurality in which individual rights are respected while diverse and various groups of people have the right to engage in political disagreements with one another, resolved by a system of votes where the majority of the voters chooses who wins the debate. Democracy is the only system in which there can be different political factions who vehemently disagree and yet not have constant bloodshed and political violence, because you fight at the polls, not in the streets. Democracy is based upon conceding to other human beings the dignity and respect to believe that they have the right to participate in politics alongside you, even if they disagree with you.

Some crazy Libertarians honestly believe that a Far Right

dictatorship would be superior to democracy, because it would prevent the Far Left from ever being able to impose Communism, and it would create, and protect, capitalism and economic freedom. Or they want a Far Right uprising, because they would honestly prefer to resolve all political arguments by means of a gun, with armed fighting in the streets, and chaos, instead of by means of a civil, peaceful, orderly political process, in a democracy, governed by the rule of law.

But, even though I am a vehement Anti-Communist, I want a system where the Far Left can be elected. And where the Far Right can also be elected, despite the fact that I am not a Christian and I am not a Fascist. I do not want the Far Left or the Far Right to ever win elections. I just want them both to have the freedom to be able to win elections, to have the ability, but to never actually do so. Not merely as a matter of abstract theory and principle, but because of the extreme practical benefits of democracy. Because, if there is a political party that cannot run in an election, then that is not a democracy.

Why is democracy good? Because if, today, the voters vote the Far Left or Far Right shithead idiot politicians in, and tomorrow, the politicians fuck up, then the day after tomorrow, we vote them out. They will fuck up. If there's freedom of the press, then the press reports on the fact that they fucked up. Then the voters, if the voters are sane, will vote them out. That's how it works. That's how democracy always works.

But, if a politician who can actually get things done, and is actually good, and is smart, and works hard, and serves the people, gets voted in, and doesn't fuck up, then they continue hold office. Here I am talking about what happens if a normal person gets elected, instead of a Far Right lunatic or a Far Left lunatic. And then things actually work, until such time as they do fuck up, and/ or the voters get bored with them, and lose interest. And then they, too, get voted out.

In freedom, people are free. In a democracy, you can have freedom. But if you have one-party rule, even by the Far Right, then you can never vote them out, and then there's probably no free press anymore either, and then they fuck up, and there's nothing anyone can do about it. So I do not want a Libertarian dictatorship, even though I am a Libertarian.

In a democracy, it's like the lyrics that the Objectivist rock band Rush sang in their classic Objectivist hit song Tom Sawyer:

"Changes aren't permanent, but change is."

And a Far Right Libertarian might say: but the Left wants to be voted in and then never leave. And I say: the answer to that is to protect and defend democracy, not to create a Far Right dictatorship instead. Two wrongs don't make a right.

And then these crazy Libertarians say, or think: people are stupid, and weak, and lazy, so of course they will choose Communism. But we are smart, so we know that capitalist economics works best. So we need a Far Right dictator who will impose capitalism, and capitalism is freedom, so a Far Right dictatorship will really be freedom.

And my answer is twofold:

First, I would rather be free with a bunch of stupid idiots than live as the slave of some very smart people.

And, second, a Far Right dictatorship is not freedom. Freedom is freedom. A dictatorship is rule by a dictator. Being ruled is not a form of freedom. A Far Right dictator who protects us from Communism, and mandates capitalism, might create freedom from Communism, but only by means of slavery to Christian statism or slavery to Fascism, and that isn't freedom.

Capitalism is a necessary, but not sufficient, condition of freedom. Democracy and capitalism are both necessary conditions of freedom. Democracy is necessary for freedom, because, while capitalism is the embodiment of economic freedom, democracy is the embodiment of political freedom.

And then the Far Right crazy Libertarian partisans will accuse me of not being gung-ho and extreme enough about wanting Libertarianism to win, because I say that I want a democracy where everyone, including the Far Left, can participate, and be able to win elections, and I do not desire the formation of a Far Right dictatorship.

Well, to that, I might say, one-party rule is not democracy, but the two-party system of the USA probably is not democracy either, because the ballot access laws make it difficult or impossible to run as a third party candidate. Only the two major parties have ballot access, so the members of every third party are forcibly excluded from participation in the political process. Open up politics, and make it a real democracy in the USA, and then I think Libertarianism would have a very full and fair opportunity to succeed.

There are those who say that we need ballot access laws, because it cannot be a democracy without elections, and you cannot have an election without rules. While it is true that you could not have a fair election without a set of rules, it is also true that there exists no need to have ballot access rules whose effect is to limit the list of candidates you can vote on to only the two major parties and their candidates, thereby excluding all third parties and independents from participation in a democracy. If people are excluded from democracy, then that is not democracy.

In a real democracy, there is no state-sponsored political party or official state political party, because if there was, elections would be a phony sham. In America today, we have, not one state party, but two state parties, two political parties which are favored by the state and tied to the state. This has undermined democracy in America. But it is not too late to save freedom.

And the Far Right Libertarian reply to me is that democracy is a form of government, and government is evil, therefore we must impose anarcho-capitalism by force.

And then I say, if you want anarcho-capitalism, go to the fucking polls and win a fucking election. If you impose your anarcho-capitalist desires onto the public against the people's will, then you are no better than any other form of government, and that's just government by a different name, because you will be destroying freedom, people's right to be involved in and control the form of political order that governs them, in order to control other people and force them to act according to your beliefs, instead of them acting according to their beliefs, which is precisely the definition of what government is.

And then they'll say: but we don't want to control other people, we just want the government to leave us alone, so we have the right to force them to leave us alone. And only a Far Right dictatorship can really do this for us.

And I say: yes, technically speaking, it is true that you have the right to be left alone. But, if you want to be a member of a society, then get involved in its political process, and get votes to get everyone to leave you alone. If you don't want to participate, go run off to some forest or woods somewhere and vanish into the wilderness. Everyone else does not magically get forced to obey your Libertarian beliefs just because your beliefs are correct and you want to be left alone. While it is true that Libertarianism is true for everyone, it is also true that not everyone is a Libertarian. The sense that you need to universalize your politics, just because you know that you are objectively correct, is a great enemy of freedom, and is one of the techniques that is used to turn politics into a missionary religion, on both the Left and the Right. If your goal is to convert others by force, then your goal is not freedom.

You do, of course, have the right to be left alone. So go off somewhere and be left alone. If you want a social existence with other humans, then, yes, democracy is the political tool by means of which humans coexist politically in a society, in a social existence. You do not get to have it both ways. You do not get to have your cake and eat it too. You do not have the right to participate in a society yet reject democracy as the peaceful political process for that society.

And then they say they did not consent to be governed by this democracy, but they still want to be a member of this society. And then I reply, I am saying that democracy is a condition whose necessity is defined by human nature, because humans are social by nature, humans are social animals. And a human does not need to consent to having a human nature, it simply exists. Things are what they are. Humans are humans. So it is an objective fact of reality which does not require your consent in order to exist and for you to be bound by these laws of nature.

It is worth noting that, while the authoritarians understand that democracy is the biggest threat to tyranny, it is the defenders and champions of democracy who are the ones who seem to have forgotten the importance and value of democracy. The advocates of democracy fail to see that democracy is a noble ideal, worth fighting for, and worth getting excited about. People hate politics in a democracy, so they dream longingly of any escape from it. They fail to realize that, while democracy sucks because politicians suck, freedom is awesome, and the lack of freedom is hell, and, if democracy dies, then freedom also dies. Democracy sucks, but it is heaven in comparison to not being free.

Today, in 2023, not only does a Second Civil War between Left and Right loom, but there is also the looming specter of World War III, fought between the West and the rest of the world, which would probably be fought between the New Allies, the Western democracies, against the New Axis, of the Fascists of Europe and Russia allied with the Communists of Asia and the Islamic religious statists of the Middle East.

The authoritarians know that, in terms of the lived experiences of the people who suffer under them, there is really no practical difference between Fascism, Communism, or religious statism. And there is also really no difference, in terms of the lived experiences of living in them, between an Islamic state, a Christian state, or a Jewish state, or, for that matter, a Hindu state or a Buddhist state. Those are all merely forms of a religious state, with an official state religion. In a true liberal democracy, there is no state religion, and there is no state economics.

The real difference, in terms of lived experiences, is between a free democracy, on the one hand, and authoritarian rule, on the other hand. You can have one or the other. You cannot have both. And there is no middle ground between the two. The authoritarians are working tirelessly to try to undermine and destroy democracy, because they know that democracy is the biggest threat to them.

This is why the Fascists, Communists, and Islamic statists, are entering into an unholy alliance, for the single and express purpose of destroying democracy in the West. They hope that they can destroy that shining light, that radiant torch, of freedom, so that it never serves to inspire sparks and cinders of defiance in people within their own dictatorial states, so that their own people lose all hope of ever having democracy and freedom. Because their people will have been taught that democracy failed, that freedom does not work, that freedom failed, if the West loses World War III.

Sadly, within the West, who have that prized crown jewel, democracy, we the people have failed to appreciate it. We think that democracy sucks because politics sucks, even though, in logic, the fact that politics sucks does not prove, or imply, that democracy sucks. And, sadly, because we are not using democracy to its fullest and highest potential, we may end up losing our freedom. Not because we had to, but because we were not willing to put up a fight to save it, in a tough fight against its many foes and enemies.

Of course, as a Libertarian, I am an anti-war pacifist. I believe that World War III must be avoided if at all possible. However, when someone attacks you, you do not get to decide whether to fight a war of self-defense. You fight, or you die. You have to fight. Libertarian pacifism only forbids wars of aggression, it does not forbid wars of self-defense.

Freedom works. Democracy works. The USA has worked, and prospered, for 200 years. The USA had some problems, such as the Civil War, and the Great Depression, and the New Deal, and the Great Recession. Freedom has had its ups and downs. But the USA has endured.

And the lived experiences of the Americans, for good or bad, is that they are free. They choose their job. They choose who their lovers, and friends, are. They choose what work to do, what to buy, and what labor to sell in return for salary. They choose which religion to practice, and what to believe. They choose what news to listen to, what media to listen to, and what culture to experience. And they choose whom to vote for, in any election.

The people in other nations do not get to do that. They do

not have our freedoms. Freedom is an ideal worth fighting for. Freedom is good.

And freedom does not work only in America, only for Americans. Freedom is good for everyone.

Freedom to choose entails risk. If you make a bad choice, then you suffer the consequences. In a free democracy, there is no big government that will protect you from that failure. But that is the tradeoff. Less safety, but more freedom. And I know that the price is worth the benefit, to pay for freedom. Why? You would have to study, or at least skim, the political philosophy of Libertarianism and Objectivism.

IS LIBERTARIANISM LEFT OR RIGHT?

The Christian Church desires to crush the spirit of the free individual, to quell the individual's mind and quash all reason and doubts and logic, and to break the individual's rebellious and independent spirit, so that they will obey the priests, without doubts and without questions, and then humbly give their money to the crooked Christian politicians.

The Communists desire for the individual to be subservient to society, and to crush and break the spirit of the individual, and for individuality and uniqueness to be destroyed, such that everyone is the same, and we are all one big, vague, gray mass of people, society, the masses, with no unique individuality, all joined into one collective, where society takes care of the individual and society controls each individual and the individual is morally obligated to serve society, and then the Communist politicians can loot the economy, in society's name, and steal from the taxpayers, on the pretext of the good of society, at will.

To paraphrase Ayn Rand, from The Fountainhead, where she narrates a speech by the villain: "Our goal: Obedience to the state, or obedience to society, or obedience to God. What type doesn't really matter. But obey, obey, obey. Never let the individual be free to make a choice. Offer poison as food and poison as antidote. Offer the Republicans as the cure for the Democrats, and the Democrats as the cure for the Republicans. And then the people are stuck, because there is no cure." But there is a cure. The cure is Objectivism and Libertarianism.

Let me opine on whether Objectivism and Libertarianism are on the political Right, or are neither Left nor Right.

The Right means the Christian Right, the Christian statists. The Right views Objectivism and Libertarianism as a form of Anti-Communism, as Anti-Communist economics, or as an Anti-Communist morality of economics and an Anti-Communist ethics of economics.

The Right seeks to exploit Libertarians and Objectivists, and make use of us, as Anti-Communism, for our principled and idealistic Anti-Communist economics, in order to attack the Communists, because the Right knows that, today, the Communists are the most powerful enemies standing in the way of a Christian state. The Right knows that the Communists care a lot about economics, but Christianity itself has no inherent economic theory, there is no theory of economics articulated in the Bible.

So the Right has come to Objectivism and Libertarianism to look for an Anti-Communist economics, to use to attack the Communists on economics, because the Right knows that the Communists care about economics a lot. They know that Anti-Communist economics hurts the Communists a lot. The Right holds the belief that, if the Communists lose on economics, then Communism will be defeated. And this will pave a clear path forward for the formation of a Christian state, because Communism, as the chief obstacle to the creation of a Christian state, will have been defeated by Objectivism and Libertarianism.

Then there are people, such as some Blacks on the Left, and some LGBTQ queers on the Left, who believe that Communism is necessary for Black liberation, and who believe that Communism is necessary for queer liberation. But what they really mean is that the Communists are protecting the Blacks from the white racists of the Fascist Right, and that the Communists are protecting the LGBTQ queers from the Christian statists who want to criminalize being queer. So these people view Objectivism and Libertarianism as racist and homophobic and transphobic, because they know that we are Anti-Communists, and they view Communism as their only hope against the Christian theocratic Right or the white Fascist Right. So they think that our purpose must be anti-Black or anti-queer because they know that we are Anti-Communist, and they see the Communist Left and the Christian Right as the only two options. They cannot imagine the existence of a third path.

In a sort of equal but opposite way, many people in the Christian Right came to the Christian Right because they saw the evils of Communism and they learned about the horrors of Communism, and they saw the Christian statists as the most effective enemy of Communism, so they joined the Christian Right to fight Communism. But, once there, they sank too deep in the mud, and got wedded to Christianity, and got stuck with Christian theocracy, or with Fascism. They lost sight of the ideals of liberty that they had caught a vision of when they saw the evils that happen when liberty is destroyed.

All such people should learn about Libertarianism, but some are not smart enough to do so, while others are merely ignorant, because Libertarians have previously done such a bad job of being visible and making people know that we exist.

All of these people are wrong. Objectivism and Libertarianism is not mere Anti-Communism, and is not mere Anti-Communist economics. We are a third path. We have a substantive body of theory and idea and belief, which, yes, does refute Communist economics, and could defeat Communism. But we will stand in the way of a Christian state or a Fascist state with the same zeal with which we oppose a Communist state. We are advocates of freedom and liberty. And so, by our very nature, we will always oppose and prevent a Christian State, or a Fascist state, as well as a Communist state.

And so we are on neither the Left nor the Right, and both the Left and the Right are wrong about us, both Left and Right completely misunderstand us. We do not seek to destroy Communism in order to clear a path for a Christian state, or for the white Fascists. Instead, we seek to clear a path to freedom, for everyone, and for liberty, because of our principles and ideals.

Black people and LGBTQ queer people have the right to be

free from physical violence directed against them because of their identity (or for any other reason). And they also have the right to freedom from laws that legislate against them. And these are rights which all humans also share in common. And these freedoms will be protected in a utopia enacted by Objectivism and Libertarianism.

INTRO, PART II

Gender evolved in the form of a basic trade between caveman and cavewoman: Cavewoman would give positive energy to caveman in the form of beauty, love, nurturing, politeness, and social skills, and, in return, caveman would inflict negative energy upon cavewoman's enemies for the protection of cavewoman, by means of strength, toughness, power, aggression, assertiveness, and the ability to be rude and mean and nasty without remorse or regret. Because of this, being a woman evolved into the art of cultivating the skills of creating positive energy, without regard for the ability to cause negativity, while being a man evolved into the art of inflicting negative energy, while relying upon woman for positivity. To survive, caveman and cavewoman depended upon each other.

In today's modern world, however, masculinity has evolved into an embodiment in the political Right, as the essence of toxic masculinity, while femininity evolved into the political Left, as the drive to be protected from harm by society and to be kept safe by social safety at all costs. And there is a war between Right and Left, between male and female, between the desire for the freedom to be rude, or the desire to enslave those who have strength in order to serve the weak.

In politics, the Right tends to be the more Manly, Masculine side. The Right value strength, and assertiveness, and domination against enemies (in foreign policy and wars, for example), and they view government control and regulations as a challenge to their manhood as the king of their household and independent ruler of their own life, and they value the toughness to be resilient against pain and to take a beating without getting knocked down.

In contrast, the Left tends to be more on the Womanly, Female side. The Left wants everyone to be taken care of and that no one should ever have to take risks or face danger, and everyone must always be protected by someone else (by the government), and they want everyone to always be treated in a nice respectful way, with people not being allowed to ever be mean or rude or disrespectful.

THE LEFT AS FORCED FEMINIZATION

Socialism is, in essence, the forced feminization of the populace, placing the populace into a role of female weakness and helplessness to then be protected by the government in the role of male. As such, the men of the Right bristle at, and reject, all socialism, while socialism is cheered by the women and LGBTQs of the Left, and by the men of the Left who feel destined to assume the role of government with its power and authority to protect those women and LGBTQs on their behalf. Any group whose identity and sense of self-esteem comes from being a victim and from projecting self-pity and needing to be protected by someone else, would also naturally fall into the female position of weakness in relation to a male government as protector, and they would naturally support socialism.

Socialism imposes womanhood onto the public, and the socialist government claims the man's role as protector, and so the men of the Right inherently feel that socialism challenges their manhood as individuals and seeks to deny and take away their status as men, which would make them feel weak in relation to their own women and feel unable to fight their battles as men.

So the Right will always oppose any position that the Left takes, for government and regulations and policy, and they will oppose them for the sake of opposing them, for the sake of preserving their masculinity, and not because they have a substantive rational objection to why this or that policy will not work, even if, by random chance, the government's position is objectively correct, and opposition is crazy, for that particular political issue.

This explains why the Right sometimes takes positions that are crazy: they do so in order to oppose the Left, not because they really care about the issue itself. The Right would favor personal responsibility and, for example, gun ownership or the freedom to run a business, because the men of the Right feel competent to fight their battles themselves, and to win, instead of needing the government to fight their battles for them.

While the Left claims to be progressive on gender, the Left's political gender dynamic is, ultimately, merely a variation of the traditional caveman psychological dynamic, where the caveman government protects the cavewoman public and fights all battles on her behalf.

THE RIGHT AS FORCED MASCULINIZATION

The Fascism of the Right, is, in essence, the forced masculinization of a society, where an entire nation is put into a state of masculine anger and aggression, and the goal is to dominate all enemies and triumph by conquest. The fascists' goal is to win all fights by means of their negative energy exceeding the enemy's negative energy, so they want to be as negative as possible, and their strategy is to engage in any and every fight possible, for this purpose: to strengthen their powers of negative energy to be as high as possible, because every fight that they win tests, hones, and improves their powers of causing negativity.

Fascists tend to persecute political dissidents and to punish dissent, and they also tend to seek out wars of conquest, as fighting for the sake of fighting, conflict solely for the purpose of making a display of manly, muscular strength. They have no mercy and no sympathy, and they walk the path which, in history, belonged to, for example, the Roman soldier or the Viking warrior, as bloodthirsty conqueror.

The Right tends to want men in male gender roles and women in female gender roles, because their men and women still rely upon "men being men" in the caveman model, their men need to be men, and their women rely on their men to be men for them, so they become insecure about their gender roles when they face gender-fluidity and their gender is challenged. That explains their love of tradition, it dates back to the caveman dynamic, which, to be fair to the Right, is how humans evolved 10,000 years ago and how we survived until the past century.

The Left is more gender-fluid and LGBTQ, which defines them as more progressive and modern, because they are more willing to have anyone in any gender role, and they can use women in male roles or men in female roles with success, and so they are less dependent upon men acting out the male gender role in order for their men and women to survive.

Despite the fact that strength and power are Right virtues and softness and sensitivity are Left virtues, Right and Left do not necessarily correlate to Right control/dictatorship and Left freedom/democracy, it is not true that the Right is always dictatorial and the Left is always pro-freedom. Each could be either.

The freedom Right are, for example, the libertarians. The dictatorial/control Right are the fascists, who desire total control by a dictator. The dictatorial/control Left are the socialists, the communists, and the progressives, who desire total control by the government. The democracy/freedom Left would be, for example, moderate center-left tax-and-spend liberals.

Tyranny is the condition of total control, regardless of whether it is by a Right dictator or by a Left government. In contrast, true freedom requires democracy and civil liberties and a free press, regardless of whether the Left or the Right is the political party that happened to most recently obtain the most votes.

Economic freedom tends to be male freedom, the freedom for the strong: free market capitalism, gun rights, no government control.

Social freedom tends to be female freedom, the freedom to be beautiful, or freedom for the weak: things being being nice and polite and being free from rudeness and from offensive behavior, abortion rights, LGBTQ rights, gay marriage, or, as a type of freedom to be weak, protection from racism, the right to use recreational hard drugs, immigration freedoms.

The social Right tends to be, not freedom, but men attacking female freedom, and men oppressing women: preventing women from having abortions, attacking the legal rights of transgender female youth, attacking the freedom to engage in LGBTQ sex or LGBTQ identity, etc.

Similarly, the economic Left tends to be, not freedom, but men attacking male freedom on behalf of women, and men oppressing other men, such as men telling other men what they have to do, how they have to behave, forcing people to conform to safety instead of taking risks, and forcing them to obey the government, instead of just letting them do whatever they want.

LIBERTARIANISM AS FREEDOM

In contrast to socialism as forced feminization and fascism as forced masculinization, in a libertarian, liberal, free democracy, such as today's United States of America, each individual has the liberty to choose his, her, or their, gender role for themselves, and there is no national gender imposed upon society.

The Right is masculine, the Left is feminine, and Libertarian is the political non-binary, Libertarians are on the Right on economics and on the Left on social issues.

Envision a grid, where the Right side is male, the Left side is female, the bottom is Collective, and the top is Individual.

Right: Masculine: Collectivist - Fascists, Social Conservatives: Men rule men and women on behalf of men, domination, 100% controlled by men, women are oppressed, (often) a dictator, but economic freedom because that gives men the freedom to use their strength and intelligence, and freedom such as gun rights because that gives men the freedom to engage in physical violence, and freedom to be rude or offensive.

Left: Feminine: Collectivist - Socialism, the Economic Left: Men rule men and women on behalf of women in order to protect women, 100% controlled by men for women, no economic freedom, but (often) social freedom for women's rights, such as freedom from the rude and offensive, freedom for abortion, LGBTQ freedom, etc. There is an emphasis on safety, that the government will protect everyone (weak women) so that no one has to be strong enough to win a fight (as a man), and also the government will force everyone to be nice, polite, and respectful, so that there will be only female beauty, and no male ugliness, that is visible in discourse. They also champion the ideal of equality on the belief that men ruling for women will bring the women up to equal status as men, that the weak and oppressed will be lifted up to the level of the ruling class, by a ruling class that fights for the rights of the weak.

Right: Masculine: Individualist - Far Right Libertarians (Market Anarchists, Anarcho-Capitalists): There is no government, only market anarchy, so there is 100% freedom for men, because there is no government to nag them and whine at them and boss them around and rely on their tax dollars and treat them like an annoying housewife treats her husband. With market anarchy, there is no government to tell a man what to do, so the man has 100% total domination within the sphere of his own individual life, although he loses the fascist domination of men against women, because, absent government, no politics exists at all.

Left: Feminine: Individualist - Moderates and Independents, Liberals on the Center-Left: They want some freedom and so oppose total socialism, and they want some economic freedom, but they are deeply committed in principle to women's freedoms, abortion rights, LGBTQ rights, feminism, equality, and justice, and, in general, they want people to be nice and polite and respectful, and they take offense at the rude and offensive.

A "Non-Binary" is the name for someone who does not accept the gender binary or who does not fit within the gender binary or who adopts both masculine and feminine traits at the same time, or who is transgender and changes back and forth between being a man and being a woman. It is a term used often in the LGBTQ community, although I am the first author to assert that Non-Binary is the gender identity which is expressed in "political gender" as libertarian.

The Libertarian Non-Binary: economic freedom, which is freedom for men to be strong men, plus social freedom, which is freedom for women to be free women, free from oppression. Economic Right + Social Left.

The reason why Libertarianism always fails: Men on the Far Right, who embrace freedom and fall in love with the ideal of libertarian freedom, then realize that the principle of freedom would require freedom not only for men but also for women, as a matter of principle, and then they retreat, in fear of women, afraid of female freedom, and they return to fascism and social conservatism. And the men and women of the Center-Left, who become excited about freedom, that women can be truly free, later realize that the principle of freedom would also require freedom for men to be men, the freedom to be rude and offensive, the freedom to be strong, and so they become afraid of male freedom, and they retreat back to the Left, and have no place to go other than back to socialism.

People are too afraid of true freedom because of their gender insecurity, because men can't stand seeing women be free, and women can't stand seeing men be free, so they retreat back into the gender safety of fascism for men and socialism for women.

THE LIBERTARIAN HYPOTHESIS

The condition of perfect male freedom is free market anarchy with zero government: a set of conditions where there is no government of men on behalf of women to boss around men and tell men what to do.

The condition of perfect female freedom is no oppression, which means, no laws that oppress women.

If there is no government, then there exists no government that can pass any laws, and, if there are no laws, then there are no laws that oppress women or violate women's rights. Under free market anarchy, men are free from government interference, and women are free from government oppression.

Therefore, the condition of perfect masculine freedom, and the condition of perfect feminine freedom, is the same set of conditions, which is equal to perfect freedom.

The anarcho-capitalist Far Right libertarians (known within the movement as the "An-Caps") have a principle, namely, Austrian economics. But the Non-Binary "Economic Right plus Social Left" libertarians, too, have a principle, although it is a different principle. The Non-Binary libertarian principle could be summed up as: "less government, more freedom." Let people do whatever they want.

In general, when the government stops telling people what to do, in economics, the result is behavior that the Right favors. People will trade in free markets, and be capitalists, unless the government forces them to pay taxes and obey regulations.

But also, in general, when the government stops telling people what to do, in social policy, the result is behavior that is on the Left: absent government laws enforced by the police that ban the public from doing so, people will do drugs, people will use prostitutes, people will come in across borders from other countries, people will have gay weddings, people will have abortions, people will have drag shows in gays bars and express their gender identity as they choose, etc.

So, if you begin from the principle of "less government, more freedom," then you arrive at a place where your policy positions are economic Right plus social Left.

In general, social conservatives and the social Right are the ones who attack freedom in the social arena, while the economic Left are people who attack freedom in the economic sphere. Therefore, to be a "social Left plus fiscal Right" Non-Binary libertarian (whom we could call by the abbreviation "NBL"), is to be opposed to both the social conservatives and fascists, and to oppose the economic Leftists and socialists, which means, to be opposed to government control and power as such, and to be a defender of liberty.

The economic Right is men being free. The social Right is men dominating women and preventing women from being free.

The social Left is women being free. The economic Left is men, on behalf of and for women, dominating men and preventing men from being free.

So a position that is economic Right plus social Left combines men being free and women being free.

This explains why the Non-Binary libertarian, the NBL, is on both the social Left and the economic Right.

In contrast, the true tyrant dictator would combine the social Right with the economic Left, much as the Nazis did, because the true tyrant desires to oppress and dominate both men and women, and allow neither one to have any degree of freedom.

In theory, along the lines of the gender of politics and the Libertarian as Non-Binary, there could also be a type of Libertarian, on the Left, who is a Libertarian only because they want freedom for women, and freedom for the weak and the oppressed, and they believe anarcho-capitalism is the best system suited to achieve this, and they do not care about men or freedom for men at all, men are not their area of concern. Such people do exist, although they seem to be rare and uncommon.

According to this theory of the gender of politics, a person who was neither on the Left nor on the Right, but who is unique, and is not on the political Left-Right binary at all, would also be a type of Non-Binary Libertarian, because they are not Left and not Right, they are not masc and they are not fem. However, we would expect each such type of person to have their own unique politics, so there would not be one name or word to describe their political identity.

Obviously, a state is the most common form of government, but, even in the condition of anarchy, even in a fully stateless society, I would define the initiation of violent force in order to achieve social, moral, or political goals, as a type of government, and as governing, even if the violence was used only by private individuals against other private individuals. This is why the Libertarian Party asks for a "loyalty oath," that a member will never initiate violence against a non-violent other to achieve social or political goals: because that oath really means you will not govern others. To the libertarian, violent force may be used only for individual self-defense, never to govern other people.

Libertarians often use a visual picture called The Nolan Chart, which is a diamond, with the Right on the right, the Left on the left, Freedom on the top, and Tyranny on the bottom. It is intended to show that Freedom would combine the economic side of the Right with the social side of the Left. It can be updated, using my analysis presented in this essay, merely be adding

Masculine to the Right, Feminine to the Left, Collectivist to the bottom, and making the top Individualist.

However, the solution for caveman gender is not for the Left to defeat the Right, as both Left and Right assume this caveman-cavewoman dynamic; the author feels that the Non-Binary Libertarian will emerge as the superior method of achieving gender freedom. The men in power on the Left do not truly desire gender equality, although the Leftist activists and radicals on the streets believe that they do; instead, the men want power, and they think they get more power if they wield it in the name of women and against men, by ruling the economy. But the Right is no better, because they only want freedom for men, and they desire to rule women, and so, despite their rhetoric of freedom, they are no friends of liberty. Only the Non-Binary Libertarians can achieve perfect freedom.

I will conclude this section with this thought, which is that, in perfect socialism, the people have only positive energy, however, all their capacity for inflicting negative energy is taken by the socialist government, and the government itself then inflicts negative energy, on behalf of the people, against all critics and dissidents and rebels. This is why, much as the fascist men in power on the Right will censor or jail or shoot and murder their critics, political dissidents, and rebels, so, too, the socialist men in power on the Left would do the same thing, and cause incredible extreme negative energy, despite the fact that their premise is everything being nice and pretty and beautiful and one big happy family of positive energy for everyone.

Positive energy and negative energy are inherent in human existence, positive energy and negative energy is inherent in the very fabric of reality itself, in physics and chemistry, so positivity and negativity will never go away, the only question is which social and political institutions we choose to channel them into a form that we prefer, be they Left, Right, and/or Libertarian.

ANTI-COMMUNISM

Going to the core issue of the economic Left, as expressed by and in the Dems and the Democratic Party, a true Democrat would say that, no, I am wrong, high-quality healthcare can be given away for free, because, in socialism or Communism, everything will be free, and nothing will have prices or costs, because they will have eliminated money and trade completely. My answer: For someone to obtain healthcare, a doctor has to give it to them.

Say, for example, that a doctor visits with a patient for an hour, diagnoses them, and prescribes a treatment for them, during that one hour. That one hour of healthcare has costs, and those costs are the price of that healthcare.

To spend that one hour with that patient, the doctor needs to be alive for that hour, which requires a certain amount of food and water that the doctor ate and drank to have that one hour of life, and a house where the doctor slept the night before, to be awake for that hour. The food was produced by a farmer, who had costs to produce it, it was shipped to the doctor's town, at the cost of the food wholesaler, and it was then prepared for purchase, at the cost of the grocery or restaurant that sold it to him.

The house had costs of electricity and plumbing and maintenance, had to be built by someone, by architects and electricians and carpenters and construction workers, all of whom had costs.

And the doctor, to provide high-quality healthcare, needed to have gone to med school, to teach him, and the med school had costs, such as giving the teachers something of value in return for them teaching the students, to persuade or motivate the teachers to teach, the school buildings, the text books, the academic knowledge, and so on.

Perhaps the doctor needed medical equipment with which to examine the patient, and someone had to make that medical equipment, and it was made from raw materials, and some other people had to obtain or create those raw materials, and, before the equipment was made, it had to be invented, designed, and tested, by still other people, and it had to be invented using medical and scientific research that was conducted by yet other people, and all of those people had costs, needed food to eat to have the time and energy to do that, and so on.

If the patient pays the doctor for healthcare (or the patient pays a health insurance company, and the health insurer pays the doctor for healthcare) with money, then the doctor turns around and uses that money to pay the farmer or restaurant or grocery, to pay the med school, to pay the firm that built his house, to pay for his home to be maintained, to pay the company that sold him the medical equipment, and so on, and that's how capitalism works.

The price of something is its cost of resources that must be consumed in order to produce it, in order to make it, where that cost is measured in money as a common medium of exchange. And when you pay the price of something, you pay for those costs, you provide funding for the existence of the benefit that you obtained.

And, if you sum up all the costs of everyone being given all nice things in abundance, and calculate the price of it all, and measure that in money, and then look at the economic data of how much money exists in the world, then, no, there really isn't enough money to pay for nice great stuff to be given away to everyone, or to every poor person, for free, today, or every day. There isn't enough money to give free high-quality healthcare to everyone, so, if we tried, the system would go bankrupt, either instantly or over time, or the quality of healthcare would decline to the level of dog shit to match what costs the system can actually pay for. And the Dems might say, then just print more money until there is enough money, but by "money" I really mean "wealth," in other words, physical things and objects which contain value that can be consumed, as measured by their money prices, and this wealth is finite and can't just be created by magic. For a thing to exist, someone has to make it, in physical reality.

Given 2023 data, there is, at most, probably $500 trillion of wealth in the world (the data does not have one precise number that economists agree on, so that is an estimate), and 8 billion people, which, evenly divided, would enable each person to spend roughly $60,000. ($500 trillion dollars divided by 8 billion people equals $62,500 per person.)

And here I am not talking about global income, but, instead, about global income plus all global assets, so, everything. $62,500 pays for a middle class lifestyle in the USA for one person for one year.

So, if everyone were to be given wealth in perfect equality to spend for free, they would spend that money to live a middle class life for one year or maybe two years, which is what $62,500 can pay for, consume the money, and then all wealth, 100% of it, would be consumed, leaving behind nothing, a barren wasteland, ashes and dust, every last crumb, every speck of iron, every last atom of plastic, consumed, and nothing would be left.

And then there would no food, nor means to make food, because all the food, and all the seed stock, and all the farm equipment, and all the industrial equipment used to make new farm equipment, and the entire global economy used to make that industrial equipment, would have been consumed, down to the last iota, and would be gone, and we would all starve.

"You can't have your cake and eat it too," after you have eaten all your cake you no longer have it in your fridge to eat again tomorrow. That is how much money the rich have, were the Dems to truly steal it all and spend it on giving stuff for free to the poor, globally.

To spend money is to consume the value of things equal to its cash equivalent price. That is what "money" means, money is nothing more than a symbol or representation of its equivalent value in an amount of value equal to its numeric price, no one cares about pieces of paper with random green ink printed on it, the paper and ink has no intrinsic value, people care about what it means, the value that money represents, that you can spend it to consume.

If you spend $5, and use the $5 to buy an apple, and eat the apple, the apple had a price of $5, and you spent it to eat the apple. If you spend all the money, you consume everything. That is what it would mean to spend all the money, to give all the money away for free to everyone for them to spend.

$500 trillion isn't just an arbitrary subjective number, it represents an objectively defined quantifiable amount of material wealth, of physical value, of things, on planet earth, and there is not enough wealth, physical material value is not abundant enough, to give lots of nice things away to everyone all the time, unless each person works to create their own values for themselves for them to consume, in which case you give to yourself instead of taking from others, because if you do the work to pay for yourself, it isn't a zero-sum game where you just take from the $500 trillion and if everyone does this then we all go bankrupt, instead, by doing work, you add money to the $500 trillion economy equal to what you take out of the $500 trillion economy, and then each person is not a net loss to the system that overwhelms the economy and puts humanity into the red, and into death.

Of course, if you look at the actual economic data, most of the world's $500 trillion of wealth is held as long-term industrial or durable goods or shares of stocks and bonds that cannot be directly consumed; the total wealth consisting only of consumer goods is closer to $80 trillion, which, divided amongst 8 billion humans, if given away for free, would give each person $10,000 to spend, in other words, $10,000 worth of things to consume, for each person, and then all the consumer goods would be gone, the store shelves will be empty, and the human race would have nothing left.

But no, the Dems will say, this concept of costs and prices is a creation of capitalism, and, if we destroy capitalism, then, by magic, everything is free, nothing has costs, nothing must be paid for, everything appears by magic, so everything can be given away to everyone for free. Prices and costs and balance sheets and supply and demand are creations of capitalist economics, so, in an economy with socialist economics, no such things will exist, and we will become unchained by them, and be set free for a fantasy utopia.

But, if things have costs, then, just because you eliminated money and capitalism and prices measured in units of money, does not change the nature of a human, who needs food, of a doctor, who needs med school education, of healthcare, which requires one or more hours of a human doctor's time, and those things define a set of costs, which must be paid, the resources must exist, and be consumed, to make the thing, to create the value of healthcare for the patient to consume, or else nothing is there, or else the high-quality healthcare does not exist, because no one made it.

And the Dems say, if we re-educate people to eliminate the concepts that were created by capitalism, and replace it with socialist concepts, then people won't conceptualize or imagine prices and costs, and people will conceive of everything as free.

The Communists believe that economics is created by social institutions. So they have reached the conclusion that, if they destroy all the capitalist social institutions, and replace them with Communist social institutions, then they have the power to change the laws of economics. They believe that they can change how economics works, not merely our human practices and behaviors of it, but the metaphysical nature of economics itself. They believe that they can change how economics works in objective reality by means of changing human social structures. This is, obviously, a form of extreme subjectivism, which basically says that economics only exists in our heads, it is a human creation with no fixed absolute objective existence. This explains why Objectivism, as the philosophy of objective reality, is so extremely Anti-Communist in nature.

And we Objectivists say, that's fine, people can imagine whatever they want, you can destroy or create various social institutions as much as you want, but existence exists objectively, and economics exists in reality, and so it won't work in reality, regardless of what anyone thinks or believes.

The costs exist. The doctor needs food to eat in order to be alive for an hour to provide the healthcare to a patient, in any economic system. And the food itself has costs as the time of the farmer and the seed, farmland, fertilizer, pesticide, water, farm equipment, farmhouse, time and work spent planting and tending and harvesting and packing and shipping, and so on.

The only question is whether the economic system actually provides the food for the doctor so that the doctor can treat the patient, or else the doctor doesn't have the food and then the healthcare doesn't get provided by the doctor to the patient.

Costs exist objectively, because work happens objectively, and the prices of "free" things are merely their costs, as measured in money prices, so nothing is ever truly "free," although one person can pay for something so that someone else can have it for free, which simply means that one person bears another person's costs in addition to their own.

So when the Communists say they will give all the wealth away for free, they cannot. Why? Because the wealth is not free, in objective reality. Someone has to create it, and someone also has to pay for that process of creating it, and those are what it costs.

And Dems might say, but Marx explained how Marxism will work when Marxism is put into practice, and Marx defined the theory of Marxism such that it will work, and Marx said it won't need money, and Marx said prices won't exist and everything will be free, therefore, if we implement Marxism, it will work.

And we Objectivists say, Marx was free to define his philosophy of Marxism however he wanted and say whatever he wanted, and he controls Marxism, but he doesn't control objective reality, and Marx doesn't get to decide whether Marxism will work, reality decides whether Marxism works, and, no, as known by reason and logic, it doesn't work, won't work, can't work, never has worked, and never will work. And then the Dems would accuse me of a capitalist mindset and of thoughts created by capitalism, so that everything I say won't be relevant once the world is set free from capitalism and global socialism is created. But reality is real, the truth is true, existence exists objectively, in reality, everywhere, at all times, regardless of which system humans choose to believe in or choose to implement.

The Dems would also say, assuming they were smart enough to get this far, that my objection that regulators aren't perfect robots is, again, a creation of concepts that only exist in capitalism, and, if you destroy capitalism, then you destroy greed and ignorance and selfishness, and then people will behave, yes, like perfect all-knowing selfless robots, such that, if we would just let the Democrats go ahead and destroy capitalism already, then their Communist regulators would make everything perfect and safe and risk-free once they are put in charge of the socialist post-capitalist economy.

And, as by now you might have guessed, my reply is that the Democrats can destroy capitalism, but they cannot change human nature, which is defined by objective reality, and evolution, and DNA, and is beyond their control, and was not a mere subjective concept created by capitalism as an economic system, but which we have the power to know by means of reason and logic. And humans are selfish, and greedy, and stupid, and human, and ignorant, and have human psychology and human motivations and human flaws, although we also always have that distinct beauty and greatness and grace that comes from being human.

And, finally, the Dems love to point to the high price of healthcare in the USA as evidence that capitalism has failed and there should be free public healthcare and socialized medicine. But, in fact, the healthcare industry is so heavily regulated that it is the regulations that have driven up the costs and caused them to skyrocket, because state health insurance laws make it so that there isn't a free market where a patient can pay a doctor, instead, a patient has to pay a health insurance company and have the health insurance company pay the doctors for them. And then the health insurance companies jack up the prices when they pay the doctors in order to force up the price of health insurance which the patient is then forced to pay. And there isn't even a free market to choose your health insurer because they are heavily regulated and licensed and a spider's web of laws and rules and regulations limits which health insurance company a person can choose, and even when they have the freedom to make such a choice.

And this limitation of free choice lowers the supply of health insurance companies that are available to choose from. Price equals demand per supply, where demand is an amount of money spent to buy something, and supply is a quantity of values which are purchased. A lower supply raises prices. And these laws limiting the freedom to choose have sharply lowered supply. This has caused an extreme rise in price.

And then every private health insurance company is competing against the government healthcare programs and the government health insurance that currently exists, and government spending on healthcare jacks up the prices in the market by increasing demand, which artificially inflates the costs of private healthcare. Because, behind the scenes, the taxpayer's money is spent to give free healthcare to some people, and the people in the private market then have to pay more to compete with them for the doctors, and compete against with the people on the public healthcare systems. And the government spending money on healthcare drives up the prices, because it increases demand per supply.

Capitalism has not failed, because pure capitalism has never been tried. Instead, if free market capitalist supply-and-demand economics is true, the current laws that exist today are precisely what we would have expected to cause skyrocketed healthcare prices while lowering healthcare quality, so the theory of capitalism has succeeded, and it is the socialist crooks who are the ones who have failed.

We Libertarians and Objectivists would run a better healthcare system than this mess we're in. What we need is more freedom and more choices and more options, because a bigger supply will drive prices down, what we do not need is less choices and less options and less freedom, and to rely on only one option and one choice, government healthcare, which we are all forced to choose. Socialized medicine and free public healthcare would be far worse.

The government messes something up, then there's a crisis or problem, there's outrage and a public outcry, and, sure enough, the politicians start to bitch and moan and cry and complain that the voters need to give the government more power in order to fix the problem, when it's a problem that the government created, in the first place, although most people aren't smart enough to see how or why.

Dems might accuse me, in my defense of capitalism, of saying that I endorse choosing to let poor people die so that the rich can keep their money. But I have not said any such thing.

Some people dying from poverty is not a choice. It's inevitable, it's going to happen, and there's nothing anyone can really do about it, absent creating trillions of dollars worth of new wealth that wasn't there before, by magic, to pay for them to survive. Giving more money and more power to a bunch of crooks, to the politicians, does not save their lives by magic.

And some Dems might counter, then, that I am saying that, given my premise that there is economic finite wealth that can only pay for some to live while others must die of poverty, I am conceding that the government gets to choose who lives and who dies by to whom it assigns ownership of wealth, but I would rather let the rich live and let the poor die, whereas the Dems would prefer to redistribute the wealth, so that the poor live and the rich are let to die.

But, again, it's not a choice, no one is choosing anything here, it's simply the way things are. Wealth is not just sitting there waiting to be distributed by the government, for the government to get to choose who lives and who dies. An economy exists, in the private sector, in capitalism, already, without any active choice to "let someone die," but if the government then intrudes, actively, only then are choices made, to kill some people and let others live, by taking money from some to give to others.

Where there is no choice, there is no moral responsibility, as I have been made well-aware, because I am an openly gay man and I am constantly told that being gay is not a choice and being trans is not a choice, and I would assert that, similarly, the "distribution," or, phrased more correctly, the ownership, of wealth in a private free market capitalist economy is not a choice, or, at the very least, it is not a choice that is made by government or by society. Instead, each unique individual unit of wealth arises from the local contextual choices of the set of individuals who directly interacted with that unit of wealth.

The economy is not a choice. It simply exists. It is. The wealth that exists is what people made. What each person owns is what each person made for themselves. It is what they are, it is who they are, as economic actors in an economy. You can't change who and what people are, just by passing a law to say that they are not what they are, not with rich or poor any more than with gay or trans. You will not stop someone from being who and what they are. You may try, but you will not succeed.

EPILOGUE

This book is composed of material from two of my other essays, the first being "Bunch of Crooks," and the second being "The Right is Masculine, The Left is Feminine, Libertarian is Non-Binary." But I think the way that I edited the material in this book, and presented it in this edition, might be better than in those two books.